Cooperative Learning

IN THE CLASSROOM

David W. Johnson • Roger T. Johnson • Edythe J. Holubec

D0874403

Association for Supervision and Curriculum Development
Alexandria, Virginia

Copyright 1994 by the Association for Supervision and Curriculum
  Development
1250 N. Pitt Street   Alexandria, VA 22314
Telephone (703) 549-9110   Fax (703) 549-3891

ASCD publications present a variety of viewpoints. The views expressed or
implied in this publication should not be interpreted as official positions of the
Association.

Printed in the United States of America.

Ronald S. Brandt, *Executive Editor*
Nancy Modrak, *Managing Editor, Books*
Ginger Miller, *Copy Editor*
Margaret Oosterman, *Associate Editor*
Gary Bloom, *Manager, Design and Production Services*

From the Editors:

We welcome readers' comments on ASCD books and other publications. If
you would like to give us your opinion of this book or suggest topics for future
books, please write to ASCD, Managing Editor of Books, 1250 N. Pitt St.,
Alexandria, VA 22314.

Price: $13.95
ASCD Stock Number: 1-94224
ISBN: 0-87120-239-5

Library of Congress Cataloging-in-Publication Data
Johnson, David W., 1940–
        Cooperative learning in the classroom / David W. Johnson,
    Roger T. Johnson, Edythe Johnson Holubec.
        p.   cm.
    Includes bibliographical references.
    ISBN 0-87120-239-5
    1. Group work in education.   2. Team learning approach in
    education.   3. Classroom management.   I. Johnson, Roger T., 1938–.
    II. Holubec, Edythe Johnson.   III. Title.
    LB1032.J597   1994
    371.3'95—dc20   94-36938
                                                      CIP

Cooperative Learning in the Classroom

Introduction

This book is designed to provide you, the classroom teacher, with specific strategies for beginning to use cooperative learning or improving your current use of this important instructional tool. It will help you understand conceptually what cooperative learning is and what makes it work. Such an understanding must precede practical experience using cooperative learning day in and day out in your classroom. The need for this combination of conceptual knowledge and practical experience is what makes teaching the complex activity that it is and why it takes many years to master. After reading this book, you will have the practical knowledge you need to put cooperative learning to work for you and your students. You can and should apply this knowledge immediately and often in the classes you teach.

Cooperative learning helps you accomplish a number of important goals simultaneously. First, it helps you raise the achievement of all students, including those who are gifted or academically handicapped. Second, it helps you build positive relationships among students, which is the heart of creating a learning community that values diversity. Third, it gives students the experiences they need for healthy social, psychological, and cognitive development. Cooperative learning's ability to work on these three fronts at the same time places it above all other instructional methods.

Cooperative learning replaces the mass-production, competitive organizational structure of most classrooms and schools with a team-based, high-performance organizational structure. With cooperative learning, you become an engineer who structures and facilitates team learning efforts rather than a worker who simply pours knowledge into pupils at a work station. To achieve this change, you must use cooperative learning the majority of the time. We recommend that in most classrooms, cooperative learning eventually be used 60 to 80 percent of the time. While that may seem extreme to someone who has never used cooperative learning, we feel certain that after finishing this book, you will see that this goal is possible and desirable.

Your role when using cooperative learning is multifaceted. You must make a number of pre-instructional decisions, explain the learning task and the cooperative procedures to students, monitor student groups as they work, evaluate the quality of students' learning, and encourage students to process how effectively their learning groups are functioning. It's up to you to put into operation the basic elements that make learning groups truly cooperative: positive interdependence, individual accountability, face-to-face promotive interaction, social skills, and group processing.

We suggest that you read and discuss this book with a group of your colleagues so that you can help each other implement cooperative learning with real fidelity in your classrooms.

Cooperation

1

Understanding Cooperative Learning

Sandy Koufax was one of the greatest pitchers in the history of baseball. He was naturally talented and unusually well trained and disciplined. He was perhaps the only major league pitcher whose fastball could be heard humming. Opposing batters, instead of talking and joking around in the dugout, would sit quietly and listen for Koufax's fastball to hum. When it was their turn to bat, they were already intimidated. There was only one way to wipe out Koufax's genius on the diamond: Make David (one of the co-authors of this book) his catcher.

To be great, a pitcher needs an outstanding catcher (Koufax's great partner was Johnny Roseboro). David is such an unskilled catcher that Koufax would have had to have thrown the ball much, much slower for David to catch it. This would have deprived Koufax of his greatest weapon. Placing Roger and Edythe (the other two authors of this book) at key defensive positions in the infield or outfield would have further limited Koufax's success. Clearly, Koufax was not a great pitcher on his own. Only as part of a team could he have achieved such greatness.

Extraordinary achievement in the classroom, like on the baseball field, requires a cooperative effort, not the individualistic or competitive efforts of isolated individuals.

What Is Cooperative Learning?

Learning is something students do, not something that is done to students. Learning is not a spectator sport. It requires students' direct and active involvement and participation. Like mountain climbers, students most easily scale the heights of learning when they are part of a cooperative team.

Cooperation is working together to accomplish shared goals. Within cooperative situations, individuals seek outcomes beneficial to themselves and all other group members. Cooperative learning is the instructional use of small groups through which students work together to maximize their own and each other's learning. It may be contrasted with competitive learning in which students work against each other to achieve an academic goal such as a grade of "A" that only one or a few students can attain and individualistic learning in which students work by themselves to accomplish learning goals unrelated to those of the other students. In cooperative and individualistic learning, teachers evaluate student efforts on a criteria-referenced basis, but in competitive learning, students are graded on a norm-referenced basis. Though there are limitations on when and where you can use competitive and individualistic learning appropriately, you may structure any learning task in any subject area with any curriculum cooperatively.

Cooperative learning relies on three types of cooperative learning groups. Formal cooperative learning groups last from one class period to several weeks. Formal cooperative learning is students working together to achieve shared learning goals by ensuring that they and their groupmates successfully complete the learning task assigned. Any learning task in any subject area with any curriculum can be structured cooperatively. Any course requirement or assignment may by reformulated for formal cooperative learning. When working with formal cooperative learning groups, you must (a) specify the objectives for the lesson, (b) make a number of pre-instructional decisions, (c) explain the task and the positive interdependence to students, (d) monitor students' learning and intervene in the groups to provide task assistance or to increase students' interpersonal and group skills, and (e) evaluate students' learning and help students process how well their groups functioned. Formal cooperative learning groups ensure that students are actively involved in the intellectual work of organizing material, explaining it, summarizing it, and integrating it into existing conceptual structures.

Informal cooperative learning groups are ad-hoc groups that last from a few minutes to one class period. You can use them during direct teaching (lectures, demonstrations, films, and videos) to focus student attention on particular material, set a mood conducive to learning, help set expectations about what the lesson will cover, ensure that students cognitively process the material you are teaching, and provide closure to an instructional session. Informal cooperative learning groups are often organized so that students engage in three- to five-minute focused discussion before and after a lecture and two- to three-minute turn-to-your-partner discussions throughout a lecture. Like formal cooperative learning groups, informal cooperative learning groups help you ensure that students do the intellectual work of organizing, explaining, summarizing, and integrating material into existing conceptual structures during direct teaching.

Cooperative base groups are long term (lasting for at least a year), heterogeneous cooperative learning groups with stable membership whose primary purpose is to allow members to give each other the support, help, encouragement, and assistance each needs to succeed academically. Base groups provide students with long-term, committed relationships that allow group members to give each other the support, help, encouragement, and assistance needed to consistently work hard in school, make academic progress (attend class, complete all assignments, learn), and develop in cognitively and socially healthy ways (Johnson, Johnson, and Holubec 1992; Johnson, Johnson, and Smith 1991).

In addition to these three types of cooperative learning groups, cooperative learning scripts are used to structure repetitive classroom routines and recurring lessons, which, once structured cooperatively, provide a cooperative learning foundation for your classes. Cooperative learning scripts are standard cooperative procedures for conducting generic, repetitive lessons (such as writing reports or giving presentations) and managing classroom routines (such as checking homework or reviewing a test). Once planned and conducted several times, they become automatic activities in the classroom and make building a cooperative classroom easier.

When you use formal, informal, and cooperative base groups repeatedly, you will gain a routine level of expertise, that is, you will be able to structure cooperative learning situations automatically without conscious thought or planning. You can then use cooperative learning with fidelity for the rest of your teaching career.

How Do You Know a Group Is Cooperative?

There is nothing magical about simply working in a group. Some types of learning groups facilitate student learning and increase the quality of life in the classroom. Other types hinder student learning and create disharmony and dissatisfaction in the classroom. To use learning groups effectively, you must know what is and is not a cooperative group.

Cooperative learning groups are just one of many types of groups that can be used in the classroom. When you use instructional groups, ask yourself, "What type of group am I using?" The following list of types of groups might help you answer that question.

1. The Pseudo-Learning Group: Students are assigned to work together, but they have no interest in doing so. They believe they will be evaluated by being ranked on individual performance. While on the surface students talk to each other, under the surface they are competing. They see each other as rivals who must be defeated, so they block or interfere with each other's learning, hide information from each other, attempt to mislead and confuse each other, and distrust each other. As a result, the sum of the whole is less than the potential of the individual members. Students would work better individually.

2. The Traditional Classroom Learning Group: Students are assigned to work together and accept that they have to do so, but assignments are structured so that very little joint work is required. Students believe that they will be evaluated and rewarded as individuals, not as members of the group. They interact primarily to clarify how assignments are to be done. They seek each other's information, but have no motivation to teach what they know to their groupmates. Helping and sharing is minimized. Some students loaf, seeking a free ride on the efforts of their more conscientious groupmates. Conscientious members feel exploited and put forth less than their usual effort. The result is that the sum of the whole is more than the potential of some of the members, but harder working, more conscientious students would be better off working alone.

3. The Cooperative Learning Group: Students are assigned to work together and are happy to do so. They know that their success depends on the efforts of all group members. Such groups have five defining characteristics. First, the group goal of maximizing all members' learning motivates members to roll up their sleeves and accomplish something beyond their individual abilities. Members believe that they sink or swim together, and if one fails, they all fail. Second, group members hold themselves and each other accountable for doing high-quality work to

achieve their mutual goals. Third, group members work face-to-face to produce joint products. They do real work together and promote each other's success through helping, sharing, assisting, explaining, and encouraging. They provide both academic and personal support based on a commitment to and concern for each other. Fourth, group members are taught social skills and are expected to use them to coordinate their efforts and achieve their goals. Taskwork and teamwork skills are emphasized, and all members accept responsibility for providing leadership. Finally, groups analyze how effectively they are achieving their goals and how well members are working together to ensure continuous improvement of the quality of their learning and teamwork processes. As a result, the group is more than the sum of its parts, and all students perform better academically than they would if they worked alone.

4. The High-Performance Cooperative Learning Group: This is a group that meets all the criteria for being a cooperative learning group and outperforms all reasonable expectations. What differentiates the high-performance group from the cooperative learning group is the level of commitment members have to each other and the group's success. Jennifer Futernick, who is part of a high-performing, rapid response team at McKinsey & Company, calls the emotion binding her teammates together a form of love (Katzenbach and Smith 1993). Ken Hoepner of the Burlington Northern Intermodal Team (also described by Katzenbach and Smith 1993) stated: "Not only did we trust each other, not only did we respect each other, but we gave a damn about the rest of the people on this team. If we saw somebody vulnerable, we were there to help." Members' mutual concern for each other's personal growth enables high-performance cooperative groups to exceed expectations, and also have fun. Unfortunately, but understandably, high-performance cooperative groups are rare because most groups never achieve this level of development.

To use cooperative learning effectively, you must realize that not all groups are cooperative groups. The learning group performance curve illustrates that how well any small group performs depends on how it is structured (see Figure 1.1)(Katzenbach and Smith 1993). Placing people in the same room and calling them a cooperative group does not make them one. Study groups, project groups, lab groups, homerooms, and reading groups are groups, but they are not necessarily cooperative. Even with the best of intentions, you can end up with traditional classroom learning groups rather than cooperative learning groups. One of the major parts of your job is to form students into learning groups, diagnose

FIGURE 1.1
The Learning Group Performance Curve

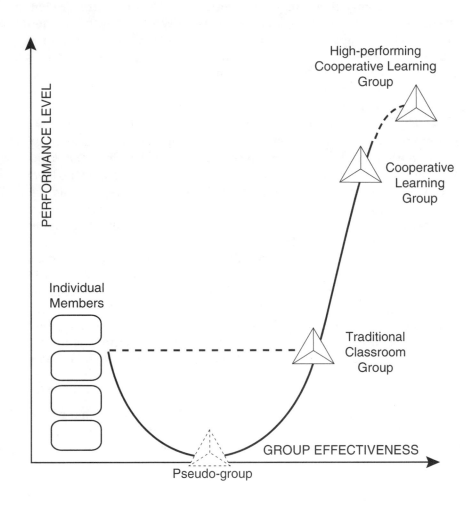

where on the performance curve the groups are, strengthen the basic elements of cooperation, and move the groups up the performance curve until they are truly cooperative learning groups.

How Can You Make Cooperation Work?

Together we stand, divided we fall.
—Watchword of the American Revolution

To structure lessons so students do in fact work cooperatively with each other, you must understand the basic elements that make cooperation work. Mastering the basic elements of cooperation allows you to:

1. Take your existing lessons, curriculums, and courses and structure them cooperatively.

2. Tailor cooperative learning lessons to your unique instructional needs, circumstances, curriculums, subject areas, and students.

3. Diagnose the problems some students may have in working together and intervene to increase learning groups' effectiveness.

For cooperation to work well, you must explicitly structure five essential elements in each lesson (see Figure 1.2).

The first and most important element of cooperative learning is positive interdependence. You must provide a clear task and a group goal so that students know they sink or swim together. Group members must realize that each person's efforts benefit not only that individual, but all other group members as well. Such positive interdependence creates a commitment to other people's success as well as one's own, which is the heart of cooperative learning. Without positive interdependence, there is no cooperation.

The second essential element of cooperative learning is individual and group accountability. The group must be accountable for achieving its goals, and each member must be accountable for contributing a fair share of the work. No one can "hitchhike" on the work of others. The group has to be clear about its goals and be able to measure (a) its progress toward achieving them and (b) the individual efforts of each member. Individual accountability exists when the performance of each individual student is assessed and the results are given back to the group and the individual so they can ascertain who needs more assistance, support, and encouragement in completing the assignment. The purpose of cooperative learning groups is to make each member a stronger individual,

9

FIGURE 1.2

Essential Components of Cooperative Learning

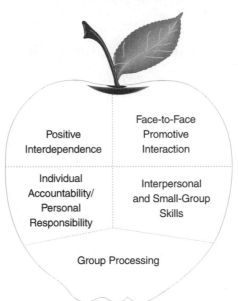

Positive Interdependence

Face-to-Face Promotive Interaction

Individual Accountability/ Personal Responsibility

Interpersonal and Small-Group Skills

Group Processing

that is, students learn together so that they can subsequently perform better as individuals.

The third essential element of cooperative learning is promotive interaction, preferably face-to-face. Students need to do real work together in which they promote each other's success by sharing resources and helping, supporting, encouraging, and praising each other's efforts to learn. Cooperative learning groups are both an academic support system and a personal support system. Some important cognitive activities and interpersonal dynamics occur only when students promote each other's learning by orally explaining how to solve problems, discussing the nature of the concepts being learned, teaching one's knowledge to classmates, and connecting present and past learning. Through promoting each other's learning face-to-face, members become personally committed to each other as well as to their mutual goals.

The fourth essential element of cooperative learning is teaching students some necessary interpersonal and small-group skills. Cooperative learning is inherently more complex than competitive or individualistic learning because it requires students to learn academic subject matter (taskwork) as well as the interpersonal and small-group skills required to function as part of a group (teamwork). Group members must know how to provide effective leadership, make decisions, build trust, communicate, and manage conflict, and be motivated to do so. You must teach teamwork skills just as purposefully and precisely as academic skills. Because cooperation and conflict are interrelated (see Johnson and Johnson 1991, 1992), the procedures and skills for managing conflicts constructively are especially important for the long-term success of learning groups. (Procedures and strategies for teaching students social skills can be found in Johnson [1991, 1993] and Johnson and F. Johnson [1994].)

The fifth essential component of cooperative learning is group processing. Group processing exists when group members discuss how well they are achieving their goals and maintaining effective working relationships. Groups need to describe what member actions are helpful and unhelpful and make decisions about what behaviors to continue or change. Continuous improvement of the learning process results from the careful analysis of how members are working together and how group effectiveness can be enhanced.

Using cooperative learning requires disciplined action on your part. The five basic elements are not just characteristics of good cooperative learning groups. They are a discipline that must be rigorously applied to produce the conditions for effective cooperative action.

Why Use Cooperative Learning?

A conviction to use cooperative learning results from knowing the research. Since the first research study in 1898, nearly 600 experimental and over 100 correlational studies have been conducted on cooperative, competitive, and individualistic efforts to learn (see Johnson and Johnson 1989 for a complete review of these studies). The multiple outcomes studied can be classified into three major categories (see Figure 1.3): efforts to achieve, positive relationships, and psychological health.

From the research, we know that cooperation, compared with competitive and individualistic efforts, typically results in:

1. Greater Efforts to Achieve: This includes higher achievement and greater productivity by all students (high-, medium-, and low-achievers), long-term retention, intrinsic motivation, achievement motivation, time on task, higher-level reasoning, and critical thinking.

2. More Positive Relationships Among Students: This includes increases in esprit de corps, caring and committed relationships, personal and academic support, valuing of diversity, and cohesion.

3. Greater Psychological Health: This includes general psychological adjustment, ego strength, social development, social competencies, self-esteem, self-identity, and ability to cope with adversity and stress.

The powerful effects that cooperation has on so many important outcomes separate cooperative learning from other instructional methods and make it one of the most important tools for ensuring student success.

FIGURE 1.3

Outcomes of Cooperation

The Underlying Organizational Structure

The issue of cooperation among students is part of a larger issue of the organizational structure of schools (Johnson and F. Johnson 1994). W. Edwards Deming, J. Juran, and other founders of the quality movement have stated that more than 85 percent of the behavior of members of an organization is directly attributable to the organization's structure, not to the nature of the individuals involved. Your classroom is no exception. If competitive or individualistic learning dominates your classroom, your students will behave accordingly, even if you temporarily put them in cooperative groups. If cooperative learning dominates your classroom, your students will behave accordingly, and a true learning community will result.

For decades schools have functioned as mass-production organizations that divide work into component parts (1st grade, 2nd grade, English, social studies, science) performed by teachers isolated from their colleagues, working alone in their own rooms, with their own students and their own curriculum materials. Such a system views students as interchangeable parts in the education machine, who can be assigned to any teacher. Using cooperative learning the majority of the time allows you to change your classroom from this mass-production model to a team-based, high-performance model. In other words, cooperation is more than an instructional procedure. It's a basic shift in organizational structure that affects all aspects of classroom life.

How Can You Gain Expertise in Cooperative Learning?

Expertise is reflected in a person's proficiency, adroitness, competence, and skill in doing something. Gaining expertise in using cooperative learning is not a quick process. Natural talent alone is not enough to make a great teacher. Being well trained in how to use cooperative learning and unusually well disciplined in structuring the five basic elements in every lesson are also necessary. Expertise in structuring cooperative efforts is reflected in your ability to:

1. Take any lesson in any subject area with any level student and structure it cooperatively.

2. Use cooperative learning (at a routine-use level) 60 to 80 percent of the time.

3. Describe precisely what you are doing and why to communicate to others the nature and advantages of cooperative learning and teach colleagues how to implement cooperative learning.

4. Apply the principles of cooperation to other settings, such as collegial relationships and faculty meetings.

Such expertise is gained through a progressive-refinement procedure of (a) teaching a cooperative lesson, (b) assessing how well it went, (c) reflecting on how cooperation could have been better structured, (d) teaching an improved cooperative lesson, (e) assessing how well it went, and so forth. Thus, you gain experience in an incremental, step-by-step manner.

As you progressively refine your ability to use cooperative learning effectively, seek the help of colleagues and help them as well. We know that to learn a moderately difficult teaching strategy might require teachers to participate in between 20 and 30 hours of instruction in its theory, 15 to 20 demonstrations using it with different students and subjects, and an additional 10 to 15 coaching sessions to attain higher-level skills. Expertise in a more difficult teaching strategy, like cooperative learning, might require several years of training and practice. Transfer (trying out cooperative learning in your classroom) and maintenance (long-term use of cooperative learning) are important keys to gaining expertise. As Aristotle said, "For things we have to learn before we can do them, we learn by doing them." You have to do cooperative learning for some time before you begin to gain real expertise.

Pre-instructional Decisions

2

Selecting Instructional Materials and Objectives

Every cooperative lesson has both academic objectives, which define what students are to learn, and social skills objectives, which set out the interpersonal and small-group skills students will learn to cooperate effectively with each other.

Instructional Materials

When planning a lesson, you must decide what materials are necessary for students to work cooperatively. Basically, cooperative learning requires the same curriculum materials as a competitive or individualistic lesson, but some variations in how materials are distributed can increase cooperation among students. When students are working in groups, you might choose to give each student a complete set of instructional materials. For example, each group member may need a copy of a passage or chapter to read, reread, and refer to while answering questions and making interpretations about its content. Or you might choose to give each group one set of materials.

Resource Interdependence

Limiting the resources given to each group is one way to create positive interdependence. It forces students to work together to be successful. This is especially effective the first few times a group meets. Initially, students may tend to work separately if each member has a set of materials. Giving one story to each pair of students ensures that they sit side-by-side and put their heads together. Distributing one pencil and sheet of paper to each pair ensures that students decide when and what to write together. And having groups share one microscope ensures that they share experiences and come to a consensus about what they observe. One variation of resource interdependence is to use a combination of individual and group materials for a lesson. You might give each group only one set of questions to answer together about a story but give each group member a copy of the story.

The Jigsaw Method

You can also make students interdependent by arranging information like a jigsaw puzzle. With this method, each student gets part of the information needed to complete the task. Group members are responsible for mastering their information, teaching it to the rest of the group, and learning the information presented by other group members. For example, you can ask each group to write a biography of Abe Lincoln. Provide each group member with specific information about a period of Lincoln's life. Each group member is then responsible for learning about one period of Lincoln's life and sharing it with the rest of the group so they can produce a report about his entire life. Because each member needs the resources of the other members to complete the assignment successfully, resource interdependence exists among group members. Each member must participate for the group to succeed.

One variation of the jigsaw puzzle idea is to divide the equipment necessary to complete a task among group members. In a science class, for example, you can give one student a microscope, one the materials to make a slide, and another a field kit to gather samples. The group would then be responsible for creating slides of collected bugs. The students are interdependent because of the division of the materials they need to complete the assignment.

Group members can also make separate contributions to a joint product. For example, you can ask each member to contribute a sentence to a paragraph, an article to a newsletter, or a chapter to a book.

FIGURE 2.1
Jigsaw of Information
Jigsaw Procedure

When you have information you need to communicate to students, an alternative to lecturing is a procedure for structuring cooperative learning groups called **jigsaw** (Aronson 1978).

Task: Think of a reading assignment you will give in the near future. Divide the assignment into three parts. Plan how you will use the jigsaw procedure. Script out exactly what you will say to your class in using each part of the jigsaw procedure.

Procedure: One way to structure positive interdependence among group members is to use the jigsaw method of creating resource interdependence. The steps for structuring a jigsaw lesson are:

1. **Cooperative Groups:** Distribute a set of materials to each group. The set needs to be divisible by the number of members of the group. Give each member one part of the set of materials.

2. **Preparation Pairs:** Assign students the cooperative task of meeting with a classmate in another learning group who has the same section of the material to complete two tasks:

   a. Learning and becoming an expert on their material.

   b. Planning how to teach the material to the other members of their groups.

3. **Practice Pairs:** Assign students the cooperative task of meeting with a classmate in another group who has learned the same material to share ideas about how the material might best be taught. The best ideas from each pair member are incorporated into each member's presentation.

4. **Cooperative Groups:** Assign students the cooperative tasks of:

   a. Teaching their area of expertise to the other group members.

   b. Learning the material being taught by the other members.

5. **Evaluation:** Assess students' degree of mastery of all the material. Reward the groups whose members all reach the preset criterion of excellence.

Teams-Games-Tournaments

DeVries and Edwards (1974) introduced an intergroup tournament procedure called Teams-Games-Tournaments to compare the level of achievement among cooperative learning groups. When using Teams-Games-Tournaments, you should place students in heterogeneous ability cooperative learning teams and charge students with ensuring that all group members master the assigned material. Group members study the material together.

After the material has been studied, the tournament can begin. You will need a set of test questions (each written on a card), an answer sheet, and a set of procedures and rules. You will need to assign each student to a triad consisting of students from two other learning groups who are similar in achievement (based on history). Place a deck of cards with test questions covering the material learned in the cooperative groups in the center of each triad. Then have students take turns drawing a card and answering the question. If the answer is correct, the student keeps the card. If the answer is incorrect, the card is placed on the bottom of the deck. The rules state that students can challenge one another's answer if they believe an answer is incorrect. If the challenger is right, he gets the card. The triad member who gets the most cards wins and receives six points, second place receives four points, and third place receives two points. Students take the number of points they won in the tournament triads back to the cooperative learning groups and add the points together. The cooperative learning group with the highest number of points wins.

Careful arrangement of instructional materials can help you avoid a number of problems and problem behaviors, including:

1. The uninvolved group member. You can ensure the involvement of all students by jigsawing information or materials. Giving each member a different-colored pen, for example, makes it possible to note which group members are contributing to a written task.

2. The domineering group member. To keep one student from dominating a group discussion, you can define involvement more strictly by jigsawing the information and materials.

3. Members seated too far apart to work together. Giving one set of materials to a whole group requires them to sit close together.

Ultimately, the choice of how to distribute materials for a lesson is determined by the type of task and what the students will be doing

FIGURE 2.2
Intergroup Tournaments
Rules of Play

A. To start the game, shuffle the cards and place them face down on the table. Play is in a clockwise rotation.

B. To play, each player in turn takes the top card from the deck, reads it aloud, and responds in one of two ways:

   1. Says he does not know or is not sure of the answer and asks if another player wants to answer. If no one wants to answer, the card is placed on the bottom of the deck. If a player answers, he follows the procedure below.

   2. Answers the question immediately and asks if anyone wants to challenge the answer. The player to his right has the first chance to challenge. If she does not wish to challenge, then the player to her right may challenge.

      a. If there is no challenge, another player should check the answer:

         1. If the answer is correct, the player keeps the card.

         2. If the answer is incorrect, the player must place the card on the bottom of the deck.

      b. If there is a challenge and the challenger decides not to answer, the answer is checked. If the original answer is wrong, the player must place the card on the bottom of the deck.

      c. If there is a challenge and the challenger gives an answer, the answer is checked.

         1. If the challenger is correct, she receives the card.

         2. If the challenger is incorrect and the original answer is correct, the challenger must place one of the cards already won (if any) on the bottom of the deck.

         3. If both answers are incorrect, the card is placed on the bottom of the deck.

C. The game ends when there are no more cards in the deck. The player with the most cards wins.

during the lesson. Imagine how students might work in the group and think about how necessary it would be to see or refer to the materials. When a group is mature and experienced and group members have a high level of interpersonal and small-group skills, you may not have to arrange materials in any specific way. But when a group is new or when members are not very skilled, you may wish to distribute materials in carefully planned ways to communicate that the assignment is to be a joint (not individual) effort.

Social Skills Objectives

When setting social skills objectives, you can choose a particular social skill in a number of ways:

1. Monitor the learning groups and diagnose specific problems students are having working with each other and then teach a social skill students can use to solve the problem.

2. Ask students which social skills would improve their teamwork, and teach one of the skills they suggest.

3. Keep a list of social skills you want to systematically teach to every class. (Some lessons require specific social skills as part of completing the assignment. In such cases, you might have to vary the order in which you teach specific skills.)

4. Before implementing a lesson, draw a flow chart (see Figure 2.3) of how the groups can complete the assignment and maximize the learning of each member. A flow chart is a simple yet powerful visual tool to display all the steps in an assignment, which might suggest or even require certain social skills.

You can create a flow chart by:

a. Clearly defining where the learning process begins and ends and the inputs and outputs. This is known as defining the boundaries.

b. Identifying all the steps the process actually follows (the key steps, who is involved, and who does what when).

c. Drawing the steps in sequence.

d. Observing what the group actually does.

e. Comparing actual performance with the flow chart. Either revise the flow chart or plan how to increase the quality with which group members engage in each step.

Students may continually revise the flow chart as they refine and streamline their efforts.

FIGURE 2.3

Flow Chart
Skills Required to Pair Read a Passage
and Answer Comprehension Questions

Understanding the Passage

    Reading Silently and Out Loud   Listening for Comprehension

    Summarizing "Chunks" of Text   Listening for Accuracy of Summary

    Relating Information to What Students Already Know

Generating Alternative Answers

    Contributing Ideas   Encouraging Each Other's Participation

---

Analyzing the Passage

    Checking for Understanding   Encouraging Each Other's Participation

    Clarifying Each Other's Ideas   Challenging Each Other's Ideas

    Summarizing the Ideas

Agreeing on Best Answers

    Seeking Consensus   Summarizing Possible Alternatives

Mastering Content of Passage

    Checking for Understanding

3

Assigning Students to Groups

Three of the pre-instructional decisions you must make are how large each learning group will be, how to assign students to groups, and how long the groups will exist.

Deciding on the Size of the Group

There is no ideal size for a cooperative learning group. The right size depends on each lesson's objectives, students' ages and experience working in teams, the available curriculum materials and equipment, and the time limits for the lesson. While cooperative learning groups typically range in size from two to four, the basic rule of thumb is, "The smaller the better." When in doubt, assign students to pairs or triads. Each time you select group sizes, remember:.

1. As the size of the learning group increases, the range of abilities, expertise, and skills and the number of minds available for acquiring and processing information increase, as does the diversity of viewpoints. With the addition of each group member, the resources to help the group succeed increase.

2. The larger the group, the more skillful group members must be at providing everyone a chance to speak, coordinating group members' actions, reaching a consensus, ensuring explanation and elaboration of the material being learned, keeping all members on task, and maintaining good working relationships. Within a pair, students must manage only two interactions. Within a group of three, there are six interactions

to manage. Within a group of four, there are twelve interactions to manage. As the number of interactions increases, so do the interpersonal and small-group skills required to manage them.

Few students initially have the social skills needed for effective group functioning, even for small groups. Many teachers make the mistake of having students work in groups with four, five, or six members before the students have the skills to do so competently.

3. As group size increases, there is a decrease in face-to-face interaction among teammates and a reduced sense of intimacy. What results is often a less cohesive group and lower individual responsibility to contribute to the success of the group.

4. The shorter the period of time available, the smaller the learning group should be. If there is only a brief period of time available for a lesson, pairs will be most effective because they take less time to get organized, operate more quickly, and provide more "air time" for each member.

5. The smaller the group, the more difficult it is for students to hitchhike and not contribute their share of the work. Small groups increase the visibility of students' efforts and make students more accountable, thus ensuring the active involvement of all students.

6. The smaller the group, the easier it is to identify any difficulties students might have working together. Leadership struggles, unresolved conflicts among group members, issues over power and control, and other problems sometimes associated with students working together are more visible and more easily fixed in small groups.

Assigning Students to Groups

A group's productivity is determined by its members' teamwork skills. Time spent training students to work together effectively will pay off more in terms of productivity than time invested in trying to group specific students together. Once students have learned how to work together, assigning them to groups can be done in several ways.

Before you assign students to groups, however, you must decide whether the learning groups should be homogeneous or heterogeneous. You might sometimes choose to use cooperative learning groups homogeneous in ability to teach specific skills or to achieve certain instructional objectives. Generally, however, heterogeneous groups are preferable. Groups composed of students with diverse backgrounds, abilities, and interests expose students to multiple perspectives and problem-solving methods and generate more cognitive disequilibrium, which is necessary to stimulate students' learning and cognitive development. Heterogeneous groups tend to promote more elaborative thinking, more frequent giving and receiving of explanations, and greater perspective-taking during discussions about material, all of which increase students' understanding, reasoning, and long-term retention.

When forming groups, you can assign students using a random or stratified random procedure. Groups can be teacher selected or student selected. Let's look at each of these methods.

Random Assignment

Random assignment is perhaps the easiest and most effective way to assign students to groups. You can simply divide the number of students in your class by the size of the group desired. If you wish to have groups of three and you have 30 students in your class, you divide 30 by three. You can then have students number off by the result, which in our example would be 10. Students with the same number then form groups. Roger's favorite variation on this method is to have students count off in a different language (e.g., English, Spanish, French, or Hungarian) each time he assigns them to groups. The following are other variations of random assignment:

The Math Method. The basic structure of The Math Method is to give students a math problem and ask each to (a) solve the problem, (b) find classmates whose problems have the same answer, and (c) form a group. This may vary from simple addition in the 1st grade to complex equations in high school classes. As you can imagine, there are endless variations to The Math Method of assigning students to groups.

States and Capitals. You can assign students to groups of two or four using the following procedure. Divide the number of students in the class (of let's say 30) by two. Pick a geographic area of the United States and write on cards the names of, in this case, 15 states from that area. On another set of cards write out the names of their capitals. Shuffle the cards, pass them out to students, and have the students find the classmate who has the state or capital that matches theirs. To form groups of four, have two adjacent states and their capitals combine.

Historical Figures. Write the names of historical figures on a set of cards. Distribute the cards and have each student find the other members of their group on the basis of the historical period in which the characters lived. Variations include grouping according to occupations, native countries, or significant events or accomplishments.

Literary Characters. Give students individual cards with the names of characters from literature they've recently read. Ask them to group with the characters from the same story, play, or poem. Any piece of literature can be used.

Personal Preferences. Have students write their favorite sport on a slip of paper. Then have them find a certain number of groupmates who like to participate in the same sport. Variations include favorite food, celebrity, skill, car, president, animal, vegetable, fairy tale character, and so forth.

Stratified Random Assignment

A related procedure is stratified random assignment, which is the same as random assignment except that you ensure that one or two students in each group have one (or two) characteristics (such as a certain reading level, learning style, task-orientation, or personal interest). You can assign students to learning groups of four randomly, stratifying for achievement level, using the following procedure:

First, rank order students from highest to lowest on the basis of a pre-test on the unit, a recent test, past grades, or your best guess as a teacher. Second, select the first group by choosing the highest student, the lowest student, and the two middle achievers. Assign them to the group unless they are all one sex, do not reflect the ethnic composition of the class, or are worst enemies or best friends. If any of these is true, move up or down one student from the middle to readjust. Third, select the remaining groups by repeating the above procedure with the reduced list. If there are students left over, assign them to groups. You can use the same procedure to assign students to groups of two or three.

The categories you use to assign students to groups gives a loud message to your students about what characteristics you think are important. If you form groups so that there is a white male, a white female, a black male, and a black female in every group, you are giving the class a clear message that gender and ethnicity are important factors to you as a teacher. The danger is that making these categories salient may cue students' stereotypes and prejudices. The general rule is that if you assign students to groups based on categories, you should use unique categories (such as summarizer, creative thinker, timekeeper, and library expert). Tell students, "In your groups there is a creative thinker, a person who is good at keeping track of time, someone who knows how to use the library, and someone good at summarizing all the ideas suggested in the group. To complete this assignment, you will need the resources of each member." By emphasizing the personal abilities and talents of students, you focus students on the important roles to be played, not on personal characteristics.

Teacher-Selected Groups

Teacher-selected groups allow you to decide who works with whom. You can ensure that nonachievement-oriented students are a minority in each group or that students who trigger disruptive behavior in each other are not together. One of our favorite methods is to create support groups for each isolated student. You can do this by asking students to list three classmates with whom they would like to work. From their lists, tally the number of times classmates chose each student. You can then identify the classroom isolates (students not chosen by any of their classmates). These are the "at-risk" students who need your help. Assign the most socially isolated student to a group with two of the most skillful, popular, supportive, and caring students in the class. Then determine the second most isolated student and do the same. In this way you optimize the likelihood that the isolated students will become involved in the learning activities and build positive relationships with classmates so that no student feels left out, rejected, or unwelcome.

Self-Selected Groups

The least recommended procedure for grouping is student self-selection. Student-selected groups are often homogeneous, with high-achieving students working together, white students working together, minority students working together, males working together, and so forth. This leads to more off-task behavior and eliminates the opportunity for students to expand their circles. A useful modification of the "select your own group" method is to have students list several classmates they would like to work with and place them in a learning group with one person they list and one or two other students you select.
(Additional methods for assigning students to groups and a variety of team-building and warm-up activities can be found in R. Johnson and Johnson [1985].)

Choosing the Length of Group Life

Teachers often ask, "How long should cooperative learning groups stay together?" The type of cooperative learning group used is one factor in answering this question. Base groups last for at least one and ideally several years. Informal cooperative learning groups last for only a few minutes or at most one class period. How long a formal cooperative learning group should stay together depends largely upon the group and you. Some teachers keep cooperative learning groups together for an entire semester or year. Other teachers like to keep a learning group together only long enough to complete a task, unit, or chapter. Our best advice is to allow groups to remain together long enough to be successful. Breaking up groups having trouble functioning often keeps students from learning the skills they need to resolve problems. Over the course of a semester or year, however, every student should work with every other student. Letting students know they will all work together eventually makes them more willing to work in groups they might not like at first, which becomes an important lesson in itself.

4

Arranging the Classroom

The design and arrangement of classroom space and furniture affects almost all student and teacher behaviors and can facilitate or obstruct student learning. How you arrange your classroom is important for many reasons (see Johnson 1979):

1. The physical and spatial aspect of your classroom communicates what you consider appropriate behavior and expect to happen in the classroom. Desks in a row communicate a different message and expectation than desks grouped in small circles.

2. Classroom design affects student achievement and the actual amount of time students spend on task by affecting students' visual and auditory focus. The way you set up your classroom should create overall visual order and focus visual attention. It should also enhance acoustics.

3. The way you design your classroom affects the patterns of student (and teacher) participation in instructional activities, the emergence of leadership in learning groups, and the patterns of communication among students (and between students and teachers).

4. Classroom design affects the opportunities for social contact among students and the friendship patterns in the class.

5. Good spatial definition helps students feel secure by telling them where the structured learning areas begin and end. This contributes to feelings of well-being, enjoyment, and comfort and improves student and teacher morale.

6. Well-designed classroom settings define appropriate circulation and interaction patterns in the room and guide students' work and behavior (thus preventing some types of discipline problems). Good

design also allows for easy transition from one instructional activity to another.

General Guidelines

As you design your classroom for group work, remember these important guidelines (also see Johnson 1979):

1. Members of a learning group should sit eye-to-eye and knee-to-knee. Members should be close enough that they can share materials, maintain eye contact, talk to each other without disrupting other learning groups, and exchange ideas and materials in a comfortable atmosphere. Students tend to share materials with others seated on either side of them and interact more frequently with students seated facing them.

2. All students should be able to look at you at the front of the room without twisting in their chairs or being uncomfortable.

3. Groups need to be far enough apart so they don't interfere with each other's learning and you have a clear walkway to each group.

4. Circulation is the flow of movement into, out of, and within the classroom. You determine what students see, when they see it, and with whom students interact by the way you design circulation patterns in your classroom. To use cooperative learning effectively, you need to arrange the classroom so students have easy access to each other, you, and the materials they need for specific learning assignments.

5. The room arrangement should allow students to change from one group to another quickly and quietly. During a lesson you will want students to move from triads (or fours) to pairs and then back to triads, which requires that the room arrangement be flexible.

Flexible Use of Space: Defining Work Areas

Because no single classroom arrangement will meet the requirements of all instructional goals and activities, you must keep your classroom design flexible. Rearranging your classroom from rows to triads to pairs to fours requires reference points and well-defined workspace boundaries.

An effective visual environment is an interaction among color, form, and lighting. You can use visual attractions to focus attention on points of emphasis in the classroom (the learning group, you, instructional materials) and define the territorial boundaries of workspaces by:

1. Using labels and signs to designate specific areas.

2. Using colors to attract visual attention and define group and individual spaces as well as different storage areas and resource centers.

3. Taping lines on the floor or walls to define different work areas. (You can also designate work areas by hanging mobiles from the ceiling, which is underutilized in most classrooms.)

4. Using forms such as arrows taped on the wall or hanging from the ceiling to direct attention.

5. Using lighting to define specific work areas and focus attention. Directed light (illuminating part of the room while leaving other areas dim) intensifies and directs students' attention. Brightly lit areas attract people and suggest activity. Dimly lit areas surrounding lighted areas become boundaries. As the activity in the classroom changes, the lighting can also change.

6. Moving furniture to define work and resource areas. Even tall plants, when placed in pots with wheels, can be moved to provide spatial boundaries.

7. Displaying group work to designate work spaces. If a cooperative group is to remain together for a period of several days or weeks, members may wish to build a poster or collage that designates their work area.

Classroom Arrangement and Classroom Management

The way you arrange the classroom can increase or decrease the number of discipline problems. Many discipline problems arise in areas of the room that go unmonitored. Students often misbehave because they believe you are not attending to them and will not notice. By arranging the room in ways that provide you easy access to each group and allow you to monitor the whole classroom easily, you can prevent many discipline problems from developing. Figure 4.1 illustrates ways to do this with groups of two, three, or four members.

Beware of students who want to sit in the back of the room. Compared to students sitting in the front and middle of the classroom, these students tend to contribute less to class discussions, be less attentive, participate less in work-related seat tasks, and achieve at a lower level. Hostile and alienated students often like to sit in the back of the classroom, which only further alienates them. We suggest that you keep students moving around the classroom throughout a class period or lesson so that no one sits at the back of the room for too long.

FIGURE 4.1
Arranging the Classroom

Groups of Three

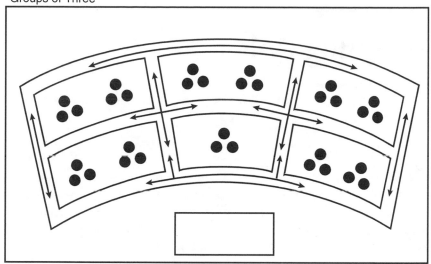

Groups of Two or Four

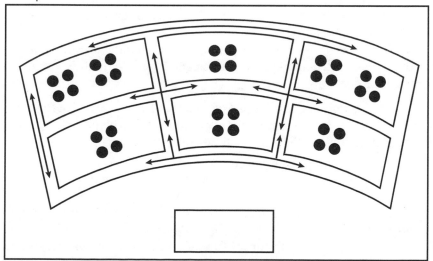

5

Assigning Roles

When planning a lesson, one of your tasks is to think through what actions need to occur to maximize student learning. Roles prescribe what group members can expect from each other and, therefore, what each member is obligated to do. At times students might refuse to participate in a cooperative group or not understand how to help the group succeed. You can help solve and prevent such problems by giving each group member a specific role to play in the group. Assigning roles:

1. Reduces the chance that some students might make no contribution or dominate the group.

2. Ensures that vital group skills are used by the group and that group members learn targeted skills.

3. Creates interdependence among group members. Role interdependence occurs when members are assigned complementary and interconnected roles.

Assigning students roles is one of the most efficient ways of ensuring that members work together smoothly and productively. Roles are often divided according to their function, for instance:

1. Roles that help the group form:

   a. Voice Monitor (ensures that all group members use quiet voices).

   b. Noise Monitor (ensures that classmates move into groups quietly).

   c. Turn-Taking Monitor (ensures that group members take turns when completing an assignment).

2. Roles that help the group function (that is, roles that help the group achieve its goals and maintain effective working relationships):

a. Explainer of Ideas or Procedures (shares one's ideas and opinions).

b. Recorder (writes down the group's decisions and edits the group's report).

c. Encourager of Participation (ensures that all members contribute).

d. Observer (records the frequency with which members engage in targeted skills).

e. Direction Giver (gives direction to the group's work by reviewing the instructions and restating the purpose of the assignment, calling attention to the time limits, and offering procedures on how to complete the assignment most effectively).

f. Support Giver (gives both verbal and nonverbal support and acceptance through seeking and praising others' ideas and conclusions).

g. Clarifier/Paraphraser (restates what other members say to clarify discussion points).

3. Roles that help students formulate what they know and integrate it with what they are learning:

a. Summarizer (restates the group's major conclusions or what has been read or discussed as completely and accurately as possible without referring to notes or to the original material).

b. Accuracy Coach (corrects any mistakes in another member's explanations or summaries and adds important information that was left out).

c. Checker of Understanding (ensures that all group members can explain how to arrive at an answer or conclusion).

d. Researcher/Runner (gets needed materials for the group and communicates with the other learning groups and the teacher).

e. Elaborator (relates current concepts and strategies to material studied previously and existing cognitive frameworks).

f. Generator (generates additional answers by going beyond the first answer or conclusion given by a group member and producing a number of additional plausible answers for the group to consider).

4. Roles that help ferment students' thinking and enhance higher-level reasoning:

a. Criticizer of Ideas, NOT People (intellectually challenges groupmates by criticizing their ideas while communicating respect for them as individuals).

b. Seeker of Justification (asks members to give the facts and reasoning behind their conclusions and answers).

c. Differentiator (differentiates between group members' ideas and reasoning so everyone understands how the various viewpoints compare).

d. Extender (extends group members' ideas and conclusions by adding further information or implications).

e. Prober (asks in-depth questions that lead to analysis or deeper understanding).

f. Options Generator (goes beyond the first answer or conclusion by producing a number of plausible answers to choose from).

g. Reality Tester (tests the validity of the group's work by comparing it with the instructions, available time, and common sense).

h. Integrator (integrates group members' ideas and reasoning into a single position that everyone can agree on).

Other examples of roles include resource roles that require each member to provide one key piece of information to be incorporated into the group's whole product; perspective-taking roles that require each member to contribute one perspective or viewpoint to the group's final product (e.g., ethical, economic, cultural, or global perspective); and cognitive roles that require each member to contribute one aspect of the critical thinking process to the group's final product (e.g., analysis, synthesis, evaluation, elaboration, application).

Introducing Roles

The easiest way to introduce the concept of group roles to your class is by using the analogy of a sports team. In football, for example, four of the roles are quarterback, center, guard, and wide receiver. List these roles on the chalkboard. Ask students to explain why each player's role is important and what happens if one or two players don't do their jobs. Then point out that you are going to organize the class into cooperative learning groups in which each member will have a key role to perform.

Figure 5.1 Roles in Football	
Role	**What Happens When a Person Doesn't Do a Job?**
Center	
Quarterback	
Guard	
Wide Receiver	

It's important to introduce roles gradually to students as they begin working in cooperative learning groups. Teachers have had success using the following procedure:

1. Have students meet in small cooperative learning groups without any role assignments the first few times to let them get used to working together.

2. Initially assign only very simple roles to students, such as reader, recorder, and encourager of participation. You might want to only assign forming roles (such as voice monitor and turn-taking monitor) until students can engage in stable cooperative efforts.

3. Rotate the roles so that each group member plays each role several times.

4. Introduce a new, slightly more sophisticated role periodically, starting with one such as checker-for-understanding. Add it to the rotation.

5. Assign functioning roles.

6. Over time, add formulating and fermenting roles that do not occur naturally in the group. Elaborator is an example. Students typically forget to relate what they are learning to what they already know until you specifically train them to do so.

Using Role Cards

Role cards can be used to help students practice social skills, understand how to perform their roles, and know what to say in a particular role. They are particularly helpful when you introduce a new role. After deciding on the number of groups you will be using and the roles you will assign to group members, you will need to construct a set of role cards for each group. Write the name of the role on one side of a card and phrases the person portraying the role might say on the other side (see Figure 5.2).

FIGURE 5.2
Role Card

Checker of Understanding	"Explain to me. . ." "Give an example of. . ." "How did we get that answer?" "Let's review."

When passing out the cards at the beginning of the lesson, you can deliberately assign a role to a particular student or assign roles randomly by letting the color of students' clothes or location in the group determine which card they get. Remember to rotate roles regularly so that all students become proficient in each task. Explain the new roles to students and have students practice them before the group starts work. Also, periodically review old roles and have students practice them.

Taskwork and Teamwork

6

Explaining the Academic Task

Once you've selected instructional objectives and made all your pre-instructional decisions and preparations, it's time to face your class and explain to them what they must do to complete the assignment and how they can best do it. You must explain the academic task so that your students are clear about the assignment and understand the lesson's objectives. The assignment must be a clear, measurable task so students know what they are supposed to do—"Your task is to read the story and answer the questions correctly"—and you can measure whether they have done it. Explaining the intended outcomes of a lesson increases the likelihood that students will focus on the relevant concepts and information throughout the lesson.

After explaining the assignment and objectives, you must explain the concepts, principles, and strategies students need to use during the lesson and relate the concepts and information to students' experience and learning. You can do this by defining the relevant concepts, answering any questions students have about the concepts or facts they are to learn or apply in the lesson, and giving examples to help students understand what they are to learn and do in completing the assignment.

Next you will need to explain the procedures students are to follow in completing the assignment, including procedures for how group members will work together. If you merely tell students to work together, they will determine for themselves what "working together" means. This does not ensure maximum learning. An example procedure you can explain to students who have been assigned the task of "reading the passage and answering the questions" is:

1. Readers read the passage aloud while other group members read silently and listen. The listeners correct anything read incorrectly.
2. The first question is read:
    a. Each student provides possible answers.
    b. The recorder ensures that at least three good answers are generated.
    c. The group decides which answer they like most.
    d. The checker-for-understanding asks one or more members to explain why the answer selected is the best answer.
3. Step 2 is repeated for each question.
4. After all questions have been answered, the group summarizes their overall view of the passage, what it means, and how what they have learned relates to their previous knowledge about the topic.

It's often helpful to ask class members specific questions to check their understanding of an assignment before students begin working. Such questioning ensures thorough two-way communication, which allows you to be sure that you effectively gave the assignment and that students are ready to begin work.

Be sure you ask the groups to generate a visible product that each member can sign. This keeps group members on task and increases the likelihood that they will behave responsibly.

Visual Organizers

When explaining a task to students, you may want to provide a visual structure they can use to organize their thoughts. Visual organizers are blank illustrations using lines, arrows, boxes, and circles to show concrete relationships between abstract ideas or events. They guide students' thinking by providing a relevant spatial format for their thoughts and can increase student participation by providing a direction and purpose for students who may tend to falter when given only verbal instructions or an abstract discussion question.

The visual organizer you use should match the thinking process required by the activity. You can display the visual organizer on an overhead projector or board and ask students to copy it or make a copy for each student or group. Be sure to teach students how to use the visual organizer. A quick demonstration often helps.

The following are examples of visual organizers:

Web Networks and Mind Maps

A web network is a wheel, which has a main idea, important fact, or conclusion in the center and supporting ideas and information radiating from it. The purpose of the web network is to help students organize and clarify what they know about a concept. In the center of the wheel, for example, students might place the concept "law of gravity." Radiating from the center are words and phrases describing the law of gravity, which the students write. The web network may be taken one step further and used as a tool for organizing and clarifying relationships among concepts. Students do this by constructing a mind map.

A mind map is an expanded web network that has four major features: (a) key idea, (b) sub-ideas, (c) supporting ideas, and (d) connectors that show relationships.

FIGURE 6.1
Web Network

Supporting Idea

Supporting Idea

Supporting Idea

Major Idea
Fact
Conclusion

Supporting Idea

Supporting Idea

Supporting Idea

The Continuum

Students use a continuum for tasks that require a ranking or ordering of material. You could give students in a science class, for example, a list of animals and a blank continuum and ask students to rank the animals' life spans from longest to shortest. You could follow this up by asking students to rank the quality of each animal's life from highest to lowest after they specify the criteria for quality of life. Students could then rank each animal according to those criteria.

FIGURE 6.2
The Continuum

Life Span

Longest

_____

_____

_____

_____

_____

_____

_____

Shortest

Quality of Life

Highest

_____

_____

_____

_____

_____

_____

_____

Lowest

The Chain Diagram

When you want students to record steps in a procedure or stages of a process, you can present them with a chain diagram. For example, you can give students the steps in teaching a skill. Then you could present them with a series of behaviors and ask them to classify each according to the step it belongs in. The stages of life, the steps in baking a cake, the procedure for driving a golf ball, and many other activities can be put in chain diagrams to give students a visual organizer for what they are learning.

FIGURE 6.3
Chain Diagram
Teaching A Skill

Steps   **Behaviors Observed**

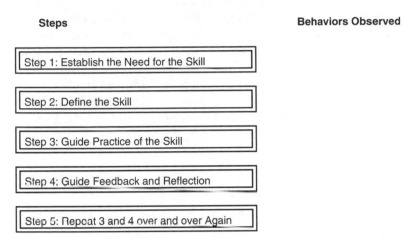

Step 1: Establish the Need for the Skill

Step 2: Define the Skill

Step 3: Guide Practice of the Skill

Step 4: Guide Feedback and Reflection

Step 5: Repeat 3 and 4 over and over Again

The Spider Diagram

Students can use a spider diagram when the task is to create supporting details for a central idea. Begin by giving students a central idea, such as polluting the oceans, and having them generate a set of categories on which to evaluate it. For example, students may decide to use the criteria of economic, environmental, political, and miscellaneous effects. Students would then list relevant factors under each criterion.

FIGURE 6.4
Spider Diagram

Economic   Environmental

Polluting the Oceans

Political   Miscellaneous

The Chart

You can use a chart to have students formulate a conclusion and then justify it with specific facts. Students can also use charts to compare or contrast ideas, events, styles, or people in any subject area. For example, you could give students the task of choosing three critical decisions that led to the Revolutionary War. They must (a) research each position, (b) formulate a personal decision based on the information they gather, and (c) justify the quality of the decision by referencing the facts. This format of asking for judgments and justifications can be applied in a wide range of academic subject areas and disciplines and can be used by students to evaluate any historical or literary event.

FIGURE 6.5

CHART 1

Decisions Leading to the Revolutionary War

Decision Made	Student Decision	Justification
Boston Tea Party		
Demonstration Leading to the Boston Massacre		
Armed Resistance at Lexington and Concord		

Another form of this procedure is to have students evaluate historical figures. You can do this by asking students to examine primary and secondary resources on the individuals being studied and give each leader a "grade" on the basis of specified criteria. After using such a chart several times, students will be able to generate their own criteria to evaluate historical or literary figures.

FIGURE 6.6

CHART 2

Comparison of Historical Figures

Teddy Roosevelt	Grade	Reasons
Issues Focused on		
Leadership		
Personal Values		

In addition to the visual organizers covered here, you might want to read about ways to use outlines, Venn diagrams, hierarchies, and causal diagrams, which are discussed in Johnson and Johnson (1992).

Explaining Criteria for Success

While explaining to students the academic task they are to complete, you must also communicate the level of performance you expect from them. Cooperative learning requires criterion-based evaluation. Such judgments are made by adopting a fixed set of standards and judging the achievement of each student against these standards. Every student who achieves up to the standard passes, and every student who does not fails. A common version of criterion-referenced grading involves assigning letter grades on the basis of the percentage of test items answered correctly.

Sometimes you may wish to set improvement (doing better this week than last week) as the criterion of excellence. To promote intergroup cooperation, you may also set criteria for the whole class to reach by saying, for example, "If we as a class can score over 520 words correct on our vocabulary test, each student will receive two bonus points."

Creating an Expectation Set About the Lesson

At the beginning of the lesson, you may want to have students meet in pairs or triads to establish expectations about what the lesson will focus on and organize in advance what they know about the topic. Three ways of creating an expectation set and promoting advanced organization are:

1. Focused Discussion Pairs.
2. Advanced Preparation Papers.
3. Question-and-Answer Pairs.

Focused Discussion Pairs

At the beginning of a lesson, you can use focused discussion pairs to help students cognitively organize in advance what they know about the content to be studied and set expectations about the lesson. You can do this by preparing up to three questions concerning the focus of the lesson and asking students to turn to the person nearest them to form a pair and answer the questions. Tell students to create a joint answer to each question by following a format in which they formulate, share, listen, and create:

1. Each student formulates an answer.
2. Students share their answers.
3. Students listen carefully to each other's answer.
4. Pairs create a new answer that is superior to each member's initial answer through association, building on each other's thoughts, and synthesizing.

To ensure individual accountability, choose one member from several pairs to explain the answers to each question.

Preparation Papers

Before a lesson, you can ask students to complete a short writing assignment. Even if you don't grade the papers, such an activity compels students to organize their thoughts and take some responsibility for how the lesson goes.

Before each lesson (class session), have students choose a major theory, concept, idea, or person discussed in the assigned reading and write a one- to two-page paper. Ask students to summarize the assigned reading and add material from another book, article, newspaper, or relevant source to enrich their analysis.

Create the cooperative structure by having students bring a copy of their paper to class for each member of their cooperative base groups (see Chapter 1). Ask students to give their groups a two- to three-minute summary of their paper. Also, have group members read, edit, and criticize one another's papers and complete an assessment form for each paper. When the group is finished, students should sign each member's paper to show that they have read the paper and provided feedback to improve each groupmate's writing skills. Cooperative groups should also summarize what they have learned from the papers and how it applies to the topic of the lesson.

FIGURE 6.7
Preparation Paper Assessment Form

Points Possible	Criteria	Points Earned
10	Has a Clear, Accurate, Descriptive Title	
10	Begins with a Position Statement	
10	Each Paragraph Is Indented	
10	Each Paragraph Begins with a Topic Sentence	
10	Capitalization, Appearance, Punctuation, Spelling	
10	Includes Information from at Least 2 Sources	
10	Includes Persuasive Supporting Sentences	
10	Includes Analysis and Critical Thinking	
10	Ends with Conclusions	
10	Other:	
100	**Total**	

Write specific suggestions on how to improve the paper on the back of this page.

Question-and-Answer Pairs

You can also have students prepare for a lesson by reading an assignment and writing a set of questions dealing with the major points raised in the reading. This results in students generating a set of test questions for their groupmates to answer. Be sure to have students record the page number and paragraph where the answers to their questions can be found in case there is disagreement in the group about the correct answer.

FIGURE 6.8
Homework Assignment

	Major Point	Question	Answer	Page #
1				
2				
3				
4				

At the beginning of the class session, randomly assign students to pairs. Have pair members take turns asking their questions and correcting incorrect answers. During this time, you should move from dyad to dyad, giving feedback and asking and answering questions.

7

Structuring Positive Interdependence

In a football game, the quarterback who throws the pass and the receiver who catches the pass cannot succeed without each other. How well the quarterback throws the ball is irrelevant if the receiver drops it. And regardless of how well the receiver can catch, if the quarterback does not throw an accurate pass, the receiver fails. The two players are positively interdependent. If one fails, they both fail. Such positive interdependence is essential to cooperative learning.

After explaining the academic task to students, you must create cooperation among students by structuring positive interdependence into the lesson. Positive interdependence links students together so no single student can succeed unless all group members succeed. When students clearly understand positive interdependence, they see that each group member's efforts are required and indispensable for group success (i.e., there can be no free rides), and each group member has a unique contribution to make to the joint effort because of his resources and role and task responsibilities (i.e., there can be no social loafing).

The two steps involved in structuring positive interdependence in learning groups are to:

1. Structure positive goal interdependence.
2. Supplement and strengthen positive goal interdependence by adding resource, reward/celebration, role, identity, and other forms of interdependence.

Positive Goal Interdependence

Every cooperative lesson includes positive goal interdependence. In essence, you say to students, "You have three responsibilities. You are responsible for learning the assigned material. You are responsible for making sure that all other members of your group learn the assigned material. And you are responsible for making sure that all other class members successfully learn the assigned material." Positive goal interdependence unites group members around a common goal—a concrete reason for acting.

You can structure positive goal interdependence by informing group members they are responsible for:

1. All members scoring above a specified criterion when tested individually: "Make sure you score over 90 percent correct on the test, and make sure everyone else in your group scores over 90 percent correct on the test."

2. All members improving their performance over their previous scores: "Make sure each member of your group does better this week than last week."

3. The overall group score (determined by adding the individual scores of members together) being above a specified criterion: "Each member of your triad can score up to 100 points. I will add your individual scores together to make a total group score. That score must be over 270 for you to be successful."

4. One product (or set of answers) successfully completed by the group: "Each group is to conduct one science experiment and turn in one report that each member has signed to indicate agreement with the report and the ability to explain what was done, why, and how."

You must structure positive goal interdependence over and over again until both you and your students see it as a natural part of any lesson. Roger's favorite way of highlighting positive goal interdependence is to require all members to sign the group's product or each other's paper when work is done. When the students sign, they know they are saying:

1. I agree with the group's answer.

2. I have mastered the required material and procedures.

3. You have my personal word of honor that all other members in this group have mastered the required material and procedures.

Other Types of Interdependence

When students first begin to work cooperatively, positive goal interdependence often isn't enough to ensure cooperation. You often must supplement positive goal interdependence with other types of positive interdependence. The more ways you structure positive interdependence in a lesson the better.

Resource Interdependence

Structuring resource interdependence requires you to give each group member only a portion of the information, materials, or other items necessary to complete a task so that members have to combine their resources to achieve their goals. Resource interdependence is discussed in Chapter 2.

Reward/Celebration Interdependence

Students' efforts to learn and promote each other's learning need to be observed, recognized, and celebrated. You structure reward/celebration interdependence by having group members celebrate their joint success or giving each group member a tangible reward for successfully working together to complete a task. Regular celebrations of group efforts and success enhance the quality of cooperation by highlighting for students the ideas that (a) together they have accomplished something beyond what any one member could do, (b) each member's efforts have contributed to the common good, (c) each member's efforts are appreciated, and (d) each member is respected as an individual. Recognizing and respecting each other's efforts fosters students' long-term commitment to achieve.

You can use two types of tangible rewards to structure reward interdependence: academic rewards, such as bonus points added to their scores ("If all group members score above 90 percent on the test, each of you will receive five bonus points"); and nonacademic rewards, such as extra free time, extra recess time, stickers, stars, or food ("If all members of your group score above 90 percent on the test, each of you will receive 15 extra minutes of recess").

Occasionally, a student resists taking responsibility for groupmates' learning and acts unconcerned about whether other group members learn. In this case, you might want to use a group reward particularly attractive to the uncommitted student (as well as to the rest of the group).

In one high school class in Los Angeles, we worked with a teacher who was having difficulty motivating students with all the regular rewards (bonus points, free time, no homework, computer time, and so forth). She finally decided to offer students "minutes of their own music played in class on Friday" as a group reward. Using the cassette tape recorders from the foreign language lab with several sets of earphones, she was able to reward groups who did good work, while other groups watched and did homework. It worked! She realized that it's important to match rewards to students, especially unmotivated students. It's also important to know that extrinsic rewards should become symbols for celebration and eventually become unnecessary as intrinsic motivation takes over.

Role Interdependence

You can structure role interdependence by assigning group members complementary, interconnected roles (such as reader, recorder, checker of understanding, encourager of participation, and elaborator of knowledge). Roles specify responsibility for actions the group must undertake to complete a joint task. The use of roles is described in Chapter 5.

Identity Interdependence

Identity interdependence is established when each group selects a name or group symbol, such as a banner, collage, motto, flag, or song. A shared identity binds group members together.

Environmental Interdependence

Environmental interdependence refers to binding group members together through the physical environment in some way. This is often done by assigning groups a specific area in which to meet.

Fantasy Interdependence

You structure fantasy interdependence by placing students in hypothetical situations where they are to solve a problem (such as how to deal with being shipwrecked on the moon).

Outside Enemy Interdependence

You can structure outside enemy interdependence by creating an intergroup competition in which groups strive to outperform one another. Teams-Games-Tournaments (described in Chapter 2) is one way of conducting such a competition.

Structuring positive interdependence is the most important aspect of using cooperative learning groups in your classes. It's impossible to overemphasize the importance of strong positive interdependence among group members. It's the glue that holds groups together and the source of members' mutual commitment to each other's well-being and success. Without it, cooperation does not exist.

Structuring Intergroup Interdependence

Structuring intergroup interdependence extends the positive outcomes of cooperative learning throughout a whole class by establishing class goals as well as individual and group goals. One way to do this is to give bonus points to each class member if everyone reaches a preset criterion of excellence. When a group finishes its work, its members should find other groups who are finished and compare and explain answers and strategies or find other groups who are not finished and help them understand how to complete the assignment successfully.

Structuring Individual Accountability

In cooperative learning groups, members share responsibility for a joint outcome. Each group member takes personal responsibility for contributing to accomplish the group's goals and helping other group members do the same. The greater the positive interdependence within a cooperative learning group, the greater the students' feeling of responsibility. Shared responsibility adds the concept of *ought* to members' motivation—one ought to do one's share, contribute, and pull one's weight. It also makes each group member personally accountable to the other group members. Students soon realize that failure to do their fair share of the work hurts their group members as well as themselves.

Individual accountability is the key to ensuring that all group members are in fact strengthened by learning cooperatively. The purpose of cooperative groups, after all, is to make each student a stronger individual. During cooperative learning, students learn knowledge, skills, strategies, or procedures in a cooperative group and then apply the knowledge or perform the skill, strategy, or procedure alone to demonstrate their personal mastery of the material. Students learn together how to perform even better individually.

Individual accountability occurs when you assess the performance of each individual member and give the results back to the individual and the group to compare to a preset standard of performance. Feedback enables members to recognize and celebrate efforts to learn and contributions to groupmates' learning, provide immediate remediation and any needed assistance or encouragement, and reassign responsibilities to avoid any redundant efforts by members. Individual accountability also helps ensure that group members contribute a fair share to the group's success.

Individual accountability is easier to establish when groups are kept small but can be built into any group activity. Common ways to structure individual accountability include:

1. Giving an individual test to each student. This includes practice tests to see who is ready to take an examination.

2. Giving random individual oral examinations. Randomly select students to explain answers or present a group's work to you (in the presence of the group) or to the entire class.

3. Observing each group and recording the frequency with which each member contributes to the group's work.

4. Assigning one student in each group the role of checker of understanding.

5. Having students teach what they learn to someone else. When all students do this, it is called simultaneous explaining.

6. Having group members edit each other's work.

7. Having students use what they learn to solve a related problem.

8

Specifying Desired Behaviors

*I will pay more for the ability to deal with people
than any other ability under the sun.*
                                    —John D. Rockefeller

We are not born knowing how to interact effectively with others.
Interpersonal and small-group skills don't magically appear when they
are needed. You must teach students the social skills required for
high-quality collaboration and motivate them to use these skills for
cooperative groups to be productive. As we've said, cooperative learning
is inherently more complex than competitive or individualistic learning
because students have to simultaneously engage in taskwork and teamwork. Teamwork and taskwork are positively correlated in cooperative
efforts.

You must make two important decisions before teaching students the
teamwork skills they need to work together cooperatively:

1. What interpersonal and small-group skills to teach.
2. How to teach the chosen skills.

Selecting Teamwork Skills to Teach

Numerous interpersonal and small-group skills affect the success of cooperative efforts. To coordinate efforts to achieve mutual goals, students must (a) get to know and trust each other, (b) communicate accurately and unambiguously, (c) accept and support each other, and (d) resolve conflicts constructively (Johnson 1991, 1993; Johnson and F. Johnson 1994). What cooperative skills you emphasize in a lesson depends on what skills your students have and have not mastered. The four levels of cooperative skills coincide with the four divisions of roles students undertake during cooperative lessons. These skills are:

1. Forming Skills: The skills students need to establish a cooperative learning group, such as staying with a group and not wandering around the room, using quiet voices, taking turns, and using each other's names.

2. Functioning Skills: The skills students need to manage the group's activities and maintain effective working relationships among members, such as giving one's ideas and conclusions, providing direction to the group's work, and encouraging everyone to participate.

3. Formulating Skills: The skills students need to increase their understanding of the material being studied, stimulate the use of higher-quality reasoning strategies, and maximize mastery and retention of the assigned material. Examples include explaining step-by-step one's reasoning and relating what is being studied to previous learning.

4. Fermenting Skills: The skills students need to stimulate reconceptualization of the material being studied, cognitive conflict, the search for more information, and the communication of the rationale behind one's conclusions. Examples include criticizing ideas (not people) and not changing one's mind unless logically persuaded to do so (majority rule does not promote learning).

Teaching Teamwork Skills

For students to work as a team, they need an opportunity to work together cooperatively (where teamwork skills can be manifested), motivation to engage in the teamwork skills (a reason to believe that such actions will be beneficial to them), and some proficiency in using teamwork skills. Structuring your lesson provides students with the opportunity to learn in cooperative groups, but you must also provide them with the motive and means for doing so.

FIGURE 8.1
Teaching Teamwork Skills

Steps in Teaching a Skill	Teacher Actions
Step 1: Establish the Need for the Skill	1. Students choose needed skills.
	2. You choose and persuade.
	3. Roleplay the absence of a skill.
Step 2: Define the Skill	1. Use a T-chart.
	2. Demonstrate, model, and explain.
Step 3: Guide Practice of the Skill	1. Assign the social skill as a role.
	2. Record frequency and quality of use.
	3. Poriodically cue the skill.
Step 4: Guide Feedback and Reflection	1. Structure feedback sessions.
	2. Structure reflection (processing).
Step 5: Repeat Steps 3 and 4 Frequently	Emphasize continued improvement while proceeding through the stages of skill development.

The first step is to ensure that students see the need for teamwork skills. To address this with the students, you can:

1. Ask students to suggest teamwork skills they need to work together effectively and choose one or more to emphasize in your lesson.

2. Decide what cooperative skills will be emphasized in the lesson and tell students why they would be better off knowing the skills. This can be done by displaying postures, explaining the importance of the skills, and complimenting students who use the skill.

3. Setting up a short roleplay that provides a counter-example where the skill is obviously missing.

The second step is to ensure that students understand what the skill is, how to engage in the skill, and when to use the skill. To give students a clear idea of what the skill is and how and when to perform it, you can:

1. Operationally define the skill according to its verbal and nonverbal behaviors so that students know specifically what to do. It's not enough to tell students what skills you wish to see them use during the lesson ("Please encourage each other's participation and check each other's

understanding of what is being learned"). You must explain exactly what they are to do. One way to explain a social skill is through a T-Chart.

FIGURE 8.2

Encouraging Participation

Looks Like	Sounds Like
Smiles	What is your idea?
Eye Contact	Awesome!
Thumbs Up	Good idea!
Pat on Back	That's Interesting.

List a skill (e.g., encouraging participation) and then ask your class what this skill would look like (nonverbal behaviors). After students generate several ideas, ask them what this skill would sound like (phrases). Have students list several ideas. Write their suggestions on the T-Chart and display it prominently where students can refer to it.

2. Demonstrate and model the skill in front of the entire class and explain it step-by-step until your students have a clear idea of what the skill sounds and looks like.

3. Have students roleplay the skill by having each student practice the skill twice in their groups before the lesson begins.

The third step is to set up practice situations and encourage mastery of the skill. To master a skill, students need to practice it again and again. You can guide their practice by:

1. Assigning the social skill as either a specific role for certain members to fulfill or a general responsibility for all group members.

2. Observing each group (and having student observers) and recording which members are engaging in the skill with what frequency and effectiveness. (Conducting observations is discussed in Chapter 10.)

3. Periodically cueing the skill throughout the lesson by having a group member demonstrate the skill.

The fourth step is to ensure that all students receive feedback on their use of the skill and reflect on how to engage in the skill more effectively in the future. Practicing teamwork skills is not enough. Students must receive feedback on how frequently and how well they are using the skill.

On the basis of the feedback received and their own assessment of their use, the students can decide how to use the skill more effectively. (Assessing group effectiveness is discussed in Chapter 13.)

The fifth step is to ensure that students persevere in practicing the skill until it seems to be a natural action. With most skills, there is a period of slow learning, then a period of rapid improvement, then a period when performance remains about the same, then another period of rapid improvement, then another plateau, and so forth. Students must practice teamwork skills long enough to make it through the first few plateaus and integrate the skills into their behavioral repertoires. The usual stages of skill development are:

1. Self-conscious, awkward engagement in the skill.

2. Feelings of phoniness while engaging in the skill. After a while, the awkwardness passes, and enacting the skill becomes smoother. Many students, however, feel phony while using the skill and need teacher and peer encouragement to move through this stage.

3. Skilled but mechanical use of the skill.

4. Automatic, routine use where students have fully integrated the skill into their behavior repertoires and feel that the skill is a natural action.

Students should continuously improve their teamwork skills by refining, modifying, and adapting them.

Remember these four rules about teaching students social skills:

1. Be specific.

2. Operationally define each social skill with a T-Chart.

3. Start small. Don't overload your students with more social skills than they can learn at one time. One or two behaviors to emphasize for a few lessons are enough. Students need to know what behavior is appropriate and desirable within a cooperative learning group, but they should not be subjected to information overload.

4. Emphasize overlearning. Having students practice skills once or twice is not enough. Keep emphasizing a skill until students have integrated it into their behavioral repertoires and do it automatically and habitually.

The Cooperative Lesson

9

Executing the Cooperative Lesson

Completing an assignment often involves taking complete and accurate notes, summarizing what is being learned periodically throughout the lesson, reading assigned material, and writing compositions. In addition to the Jigsaw method discussed in Chapter 2, you can have students accomplish these tasks cooperatively through:

1. Cooperative note-taking pairs.
2. Turn-to-your-neighbor summaries.
3. Read and explain pairs.
4. Cooperative writing and editing pairs.
5. Drill-review pairs.
6. Math problem-solving pairs.
7. Academic controversies.

Cooperative Note-Taking Pairs

The notes students take during a lesson are important. Most students, however, take incomplete notes because of low-working memory capacities, the lesson's information processing load, and a lack of note-taking skills. Students benefit from learning how to take better notes and how to review their notes more effectively. You can help students by assigning them to note-taking pairs. Every 10 minutes or so during a lesson, stop and have paired students share their notes with each other. Tell pair members that they must take something from one another's notes to improve their own. The task is to focus on increasing the quantity and quality of the notes taken during a lesson. The cooperative goal is for both students to generate a comprehensive set of accurate notes that will enable them to learn and review the material covered in the lesson.

Turn-to-Your-Neighbor Summaries

A common practice in most classrooms is to hold a whole-class discussion. Often during such discussions, teachers ask a student to answer a question or provide a summary of the lesson. The student doing the explaining has an opportunity to clarify and extend his knowledge through active involvement in the learning process, but the rest of the class is passive. You can ensure that all students are actively learning by requiring all students to answer questions about the lesson simultaneously through the formulate, share, listen, and create procedure.

During this procedure, students formulate an answer to a question that requires them to summarize what the lesson has covered. Students then turn to a classmate close by and share their answers and reasoning. Each student listens carefully to her partner's explanation, and then the pairs create a new answer superior to their initial formulations through the processes of association, building on each other's thoughts, and synthesizing. The students' task is to explain their answers and reasoning to a classmate and practice the skill of explaining. The cooperative goal is to create a joint answer that both members agree to and can explain. Your role is to monitor the pairs and assist students in following the procedure. To ensure individual accountability, you may wish to ask randomly selected students to explain the joint answer they created with their partners.

Read and Explain Pairs

It's often more effective to ask students to read assigned material in cooperative pairs than individually. (This is especially helpful when you lack materials for each student.) The expected criterion for success is that both members be able to explain the meaning of the assigned material correctly. The task is for the pairs to ascertain the meaning of each paragraph and the assigned material as a whole. The cooperative goal is for both members to agree on the meaning of each paragraph, formulate a joint summary, and be able to explain their answer.

Here's how it works:

1. Assign a high reader and a low reader to a reading pair and tell them what specific pages (passages) you want them to read.

2. Students read all the section headings for an overview.

3. Students silently read the first paragraph and take turns acting as summarizer and accuracy coach. They rotate roles after each paragraph.

4. The summarizer summarizes in her own words the content of the paragraph to her partner.

5. The accuracy coach listens carefully, corrects any misstatements, adds anything that was left out, and explains how the material relates to something they already know.

6. The students then move on to the next paragraph and repeat the procedure. They continue until they have read all the assigned material. At that point, they come to an agreement on the overall meaning of the assigned material.

During the lesson, systematically monitor each reading pair and assist students in following the procedure. To ensure individual accountability, randomly ask students to summarize what they have read so far. Remind students that there is intergroup cooperation—whenever it is helpful, they should check procedures, answers, and strategies with another group, or if they finish early, they should compare and discuss answers with another group.

Cooperative Writing and Editing Pairs

When your lesson requires students to write an essay, report, poem, story, or review of something they have read, you should use cooperative writing and editing pairs. Pairs verify that each member's composition is perfect according to criteria you explain; then they receive an individual score on the quality of their compositions. You can also give a group score based on the total number of errors made by the pair in their individual compositions.

Here's how the procedure works:

1. You assign students to pairs with at least one good reader in each pair.

2. Student A describes what he is planning to write to Student B, who listens carefully, probes with a set of questions, and outlines Student A's ideas. Student B gives the written outline to Student A.

3. This procedure is reversed with Student B describing what she is going to write and Student A listening and completing an outline of Student B's ideas, which is then given to Student B.

4. The students individually research the material they need for their compositions, keeping an eye out for material useful to their partner.

5. The students work together to write the first paragraph of each composition to ensure that they both have a clear start on their compositions.

6. The students write their compositions individually.

7. When the students have completed their compositions, they proofread each other's compositions, making corrections in capitalization, punctuation, spelling, language usage, and other aspects of writing you specify. Students also give each other suggestions for revision.

8. The students revise their compositions.

9. The students then reread each other's compositions and sign their names to indicate that each composition is error-free.

While the students work, your role is to monitor the pairs, intervening when appropriate to help students master the needed writing and cooperative skills. Whenever it is helpful to do so, students may check procedures with another group. When students complete their compositions, they discuss how effectively they worked together (listing the specific actions they engaged in to help each other), plan what behaviors they are going to emphasize in their next writing pair, and thank each other for the help and assistance provided.

Drill-Review Pairs

There are times during a lesson when you might want to have students review what they have previously learned and drill on certain procedures to ensure that the procedures are overlearned. At these times, cooperative learning is indispensable.

To implement drill-review pairs, assign students to pairs and each pair to a foursome. Instruct the students to do the following:

1. Student A reads the assigned problem and explains step-by-step the procedures and strategies required to solve it. Student B checks the accuracy of the solution and provides encouragement and coaching.

2. Students A and B rotate roles on the second problem.

3. When the pair completes two problems, members check their answers with the other pair in their foursome. If they disagree, they must discuss their reasoning and come to a consensus about the answer. If they agree, they thank each other and continue working in their pairs.

4. The procedure continues until students complete all the assigned problems.

To ensure individual accountability, you can randomly ask individual students to explain how to solve a selected problem.

Math Problem-Solving Pairs

Problem solving in cooperative math teams enables students to practice the skills necessary for problem solving in "real-life" situations. Most math problem solving outside of school happens in teams where partners interact to clarify and define a problem (identify what is known and unknown), describe and illustrate the problem (write mathematical equations and draw diagrams or graphs), discuss and suggest methods to solve the problem, apply operations, and check logic as well as calculations. Similar procedures in cooperative learning groups promote productive problem solving by enabling students to continuously test ideas as well as get and give feedback.

First, assign students to cooperative learning groups (initially pairs, eventually triads or quads as students become more skilled in working together) that are heterogeneous according to mathematical ability with at least one good reader in each team. Groupmates should understand that their mutual goal is to solve a problem, agree on the answer, and be able to explain each step they used to solve the problem.

Second, have groupmates read the problem, determine what they do and do not know, and describe the problem mathematically, using equations, diagrams, graphs, or manipulatives. After discussing and agreeing on methods to solve the problem, groupmates perform the calculations, explaining the rationale for each step and checking computations. You may assign and rotate roles after each step to facilitate the process. Student A, for example, may describe how to perform the first calculation while Student B records the calculation and explains the rationale for it. Then Student B describes how to perform the second computation while Student A records the computation and explains the rationale for it. They repeat the procedure until they solve the problems.

Both students sign the answer, indicating that they agree with the solution and can explain how they obtained it.

Finally, have groups discuss how effectively they worked together (listing specific actions that facilitated success), plan behaviors to improve the problem-solving process, thank each other for the help and assistance received, and celebrate their success.

Academic Controversies

Intellectual conflict (controversy) is one of the most powerful and important instructional tools. Academic controversies are an advanced form of cooperative learning. The basic format for structuring academic controversies follows:

1. Choose a topic with content the students can manage and on which at least two well-documented positions (pro and con) can be prepared.

2. Prepare the instructional materials so that group members know what position they have been assigned and where they can find supporting information.

3. Assign students to groups of four, dividing each group into two pairs, one pro and one con. Be sure to highlight for students the cooperative goal of reaching a consensus on the issue and writing a quality group report on which all members will be evaluated.

4. Assign each pair the cooperative task of learning their position and its supporting arguments and information.

5. Have each pair present its position to the other. The group discusses the issue, critically evaluating the opposing position and its rationale and comparing strengths and weaknesses of the two positions.

6. Have the pairs reverse perspectives and positions by presenting the opposing position sincerely and forcefully.

7. Finally, have group members drop their advocacy, reach a consensus, and write a group report that includes their joint position and the supporting evidence and rationale.

To ensure individual accountability, you can give a test on the content of both positions and award bonus points to groups whose members all score above the preset criteria of excellence. (You can find a more detailed description of conducting academic controversies in Johnson and Johnson [1992].)

Group Investigation

In Group Investigation, formulated by Shlomo and Yael Sharan (1976), students form cooperative groups according to common interest in a topic. All group members help plan how to research their topic, dividing the work among themselves. Group members individually carry out their parts of the investigation, and then the group synthesizes and summarizes its work and presents the findings to the class.

Co-op Co-op

In Co-op Co-op, developed by Spencer Kagan (1988), students are assigned to heterogeneous cooperative learning groups, each of which is assigned one part of a learning unit. Each group member is then assigned a minitopic. Students engage in individual research on their minitopics and then present their findings to their groups. Each group then integrates the minitopics of its members into an overall group presentation, which is given to the whole class.

10

Monitoring Students' Behavior

Five-Minute Walk

1. Select social skill(s) to observe.
2. Construct observation sheet.
3. Plan route through the classroom.
4. Gather data on every group.
5. Provide the data to the groups or to the class as a whole.
6. Chart/graph the results.

Your job begins in earnest when cooperative learning groups start working. While students are working together, you must move from group to group systematically monitoring the interaction among group members to assess students' academic progress and use of interpersonal and small-group skills. You're responsible for listening to each group and collecting data on the interaction among group members. You can also ask individual students to act as observers along with you. Based on these observations, you can intervene to improve students' academic learning and group skills.

Monitoring has four stages:

1. Preparing to observe the learning groups by deciding who, if anyone, might help you observe and which observation forms to use.

2. Observing to assess the quality of cooperative efforts in the learning groups.

3. Intervening when necessary to improve a group's taskwork or teamwork.

4. Having students assess the quality of their own individual participation in the learning groups to encourage self-monitoring.

Preparing to Observe

You must decide whether you will ask individual students to help you observe (you, of course, are always an observer) and choose the observation forms and procedures you will use.

Student Observers and Sampling Plans

As students become experienced working in cooperative learning groups, they should be trained to be observers. Observation is aimed at recording and describing members' behavior within a group to provide objective data about the interaction among group members. The goal is to give students feedback about their participation in the group and help them to analyze the group's effectiveness. Students can be roving observers who circulate throughout the classroom and monitor all learning groups or they can observe their own groups (one observer per group). When observing their own groups, student observers should remain close enough to see and hear the interaction among group members but should not participate in the academic task. Student observers shouldn't comment or intervene until the time set aside near the end of the class period for the learning groups to review their work. The role of observer should rotate so that each group member is an observer an equal amount of time.

You and student roving observers need a sampling plan to ensure that all groups are observed for approximately equal amounts of time. Simply decide before a lesson begins how much time you will spend observing each learning group (this is a sampling plan). You can observe one learning group for the entire class period, collecting information on every member, or you may decide to observe each group an equal portion of the class period. You might also choose to observe each group for two minutes at a time and rotate through all the groups several times during a class period. You will need to interrupt the sampling plan if you decide you should intervene in one group.

Academic and social skills objectives demand assessment of academic and teamwork efforts.

Academic   **Teamwork**

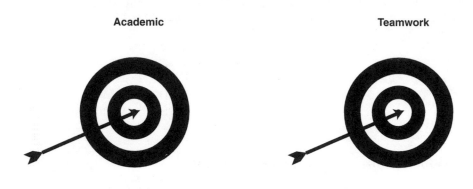

Observation Procedures

Observation procedures may be structured (using an observation schedule on which frequencies are tallied) or unstructured (making informal descriptions of students' statements and actions). In both structured and unstructured observation, it's important not to confuse observation with inference and interpretation. Observation is descriptive; inferences are interpretative. Observation involves recording what students do while they work together to complete a task. Inferences and interpretations about how well students are cooperating are made based on the observation data.

To make structured observations, you:

1. Decide which teamwork and taskwork skills you will observe.

2. Construct an observation form to record the frequencies of targeted actions. (If students are going to be observers, the form must be appropriate for their age group.)

3. Observe each group and record how often each student performs the specified behaviors.

4. Summarize your observations in a clear and useful manner and present them to the groups as feedback.

5. Help group members analyze the observation data and infer how effectively the group is functioning and how well each group member is engaging in the targeted skills.

Observation Forms

Structured. Several types of observation forms can be used. These are useful tools for gathering and sharing specific information on how group members work together while completing an assignment.

Figure 10.1 is a simple observation form you can use.

FIGURE 10.1
Structured Observation Form

Observer:			Date:	
Action	Yvette	**Keith**	**Dale**	**Total**
Contributes Ideas				
Encourages Participation				
Checks for Understanding				
Gives Group Direction				
Other				
Total:				

1. Using one observation sheet per group, write each group member's name across the top of the columns, placing one name above each column (reserving the first column for the targeted skills and the last column for the row totals).

2. Write each targeted skill on a separate row in the first column.

3. Place a tally mark in the appropriate row and column when a student engages in one of the targeted actions. Don't worry about recording everything, but observe as accurately and rapidly as possible.

4. Make notes on the back of the observation form about actions that take place but do not fit into the actions being observed.

5. Write down specific positive contributions by each group member to ensure that every member receives positive feedback.

6. Look for patterns of behavior in the group.

7. After the work session is over, total the columns and rows.

8. Show the observation form to the group. Ask the group members what they conclude about:

    a. Their own participation in the group.

    b. The group functioning in general.

9. After the discussion, help the group set a growth goal. Ask, "What could you add to be even a better group tomorrow than you were today?" This emphasizes the importance of continuous improvement in group effectiveness.

10. Transfer the totals to long-term record sheets and the appropriate charts or graphs.

A variety of observation instruments and procedures are described in Johnson and R. Johnson (1993).

Unstructured. You make unstructured (or anecdotal) observations by "eavesdropping" on each group and making specific observations that are (a) brief enough to write down quickly, (b) capture an important aspect of the behavior of one or more students, and (c) help answer questions about the successful implementation of cooperative learning. Be sure to write positive incidents on cards and file them in the student's personal file after they have been used to give the student feedback. These can be used during parent conferences as examples of the student's competencies and positive qualities.

Observing

Keep the following guidelines in mind when you observe learning groups:

Guideline One: Always monitor groups while they work. Whenever possible, use a formal observation sheet. The more concrete the data, the more useful they are to you and your students.

Guideline Two: Try not to count too many different behaviors at one time. You may wish to choose two to four behaviors from Figure 10.1 to record the first few times you observe. Once you have used the observation sheet several dozen times, you will be able to keep track of all the behaviors included.

Guideline Three: Sometimes you may use a simple checklist in addition to a systematic observation form. Figure 10.2 is an example of such a checklist:

Figure 10.2
Checklist

Behavior	Yes	No	Comments
1. Do students understand the task?			
2. Have students accepted the positive interdependence and the individual accountability?			
3. Are students working toward the criteria, and are those criteria for success appropriate?			
4. Are students practicing the specified behaviors?			

Guideline Four: Focus on positive behaviors. These should be celebrated when present and discussed when missing.

Guideline Five: Supplement and extend the frequency data with notes on specific student actions. Skillful interchanges that you observe and can share with students (and parents) later as objective praise are particularly useful.

Guideline Six: Once students understand cooperative learning and how they should behave when helping each other learn, train students to be observers. Student observers can obtain more complete data on each group's functioning. Student observers can be used at all grade levels. For very young students you must keep the system very simple, perhaps only "Who talks?" Be sure to give the class adequate instructions and practice on gathering the observation data and sharing them with the group. When using student observers, allocate several minutes at the end of each group session for the group to teach the observer what members of the group have just learned.

A note about visitors: Visitors should not be allowed to sit and watch a lesson passively. When someone visits your classroom, hand them an observation form, briefly explain the observer's role, and put them to work. Visitors may be roving observers or they may observe one single group, depending on the purpose of their visit.

FIGURE 10.3
Mystery Person

Here is one fun way to conduct and discuss an observation.

1. Inform the class that you will be focusing on one student whose name will be kept secret.

2. Observe during the lesson without showing whom you are observing.

3. Describe what the person did (frequency data) to the class as a whole without naming the person.

4. Ask students to guess the mystery person's identity.

Intervening in Cooperative Learning Groups

As you observe students, you will sometimes need to intervene to facilitate a group's taskwork or teamwork.

Intervening to Provide Task Assistance

Systematically observing cooperative learning groups provides you with a "window" into students' minds. Listening to students explain how to solve a problem or complete an assignment to groupmates provides better information about what students do and do not know and understand than correct answers on tests or homework assignments. As students work cooperatively they make hidden thinking processes overt and subject to observation and commentary, enabling you to observe how students are constructing their understanding of the assigned material and intervene when necessary to help students correct misconceptions.

You will sometimes need to intervene to clarify instructions, review important procedures and strategies for completing the assignment, answer questions, and teach task skills. When discussing concepts and information to be learned, remember to use language or terms relevant to the learning. Instead of saying, "Yes, that is right," say something more specific to the assignment, such as, "Yes, that is one way to find the main idea of a paragraph." The use of the more specific statement reinforces the desired learning and promotes positive transfer by helping students associate a term with their learning.

One way to intervene is to interview a cooperative learning group by asking group members a set of questions that requires them to analyze their plan of action at a metacognitive level and explain it to you. Three standard questions are:

1. What are you doing?
2. Why are you doing it?
3. How will it help you?

FIGURE 10.4
Intervening in Cooperative Learning Groups

O = Observe

IDQ = Intervene by sharing data or asking a question.

SP = Have students process and plan how they will take care of the issue.

BTW = Tell students to go back to work.

Intervening to Teach Social Skills

Cooperative learning groups provide you with a picture of students' social skills. While monitoring the learning groups, you may find students who do not have the necessary social skills to be effective group members. In these cases you will want to intervene to suggest more effective procedures for working together and specific social skills groups should use. You should also intervene to celebrate particularly effective and skillful behaviors you notice. The social skills required for a productive group, along with activities that you may use in teaching them, are discussed in Chapter 8 and in Johnson and F. Johnson (1994) and Johnson (1991, 1993).

General Advice About Intervening

Don't intervene any more than absolutely necessary. Many teachers jump in and solve problems for students. With a little patience, cooperative groups can usually solve their own problems. Choosing when to intervene and when not to is part of the art of teaching. When you do intervene, turn the problem back to the group to solve. Many teachers do this by having members set aside their task, pointing out the problem, and asking the group to create three possible solutions and choose which solution to try first.

One 3rd grade teacher we know noticed when distributing papers that one student was sitting back away from the other three. A moment later the teacher glanced over and only three students were sitting where four had been a moment before. As she watched, the three students came marching over to her and complained that Johnny was under the table and wouldn't come out.

"Make him come out!" they insisted (the teacher's role: police officer, judge, and executioner).

The teacher told them that Johnny was a member of their group and asked what they had tried to solve their problem.

"Tried?" came the puzzled reply.

"Yes, have you asked him to come out?" the teacher suggested.

The group marched back and the teacher continued distributing papers to groups. A moment later the teacher glanced over to their table and saw no heads above the table (which is one way to solve the problem). After a few more minutes, four heads came struggling out from under the table and the group (including Johnny) went back to work with great energy.

We don't know what happened under that table, but whatever it was, it was effective. What makes this story even more interesting is that the group received a 100 percent on the paper and later, standing by Johnny's desk, the teacher noticed he had the paper clutched in his hand. The group had given Johnny the paper and he was taking it home. He confided to the teacher that this was the first time he could ever remember earning a 100 on anything in school. (If that was your record, you might slip under a few tables yourself.)

FIGURE 10.5

Ideas for Monitoring and Intervening

Check for	If Present	If Absent
Members seated closely together	Good seating.	Draw your chairs closer together.
Group has right materials and is on right page	Good, you are all ready.	Get what you need—I will watch.
Students who are assigned roles are doing them	Good! You're doing your jobs.	Who is supposed to do what?
Groups have started task	Good! You've started.	Let me see you get started. Do you need any help?
Cooperative skills being used (in general)	Good group! Keep up the good work!	What skills would help here? What should you be doing?
A specific cooperative skill being used	Good encouraging! Good paraphrasing!	Who can encourage Edye? Repeat in your own words what Edye just said.
Academic work being done well	You are following the procedure for this assignment. Good job!	You need more extensive answers. Let me explain how to do this again.
Members ensuring individual accountability	You're making sure everyone understands. Good work!	Roger, show me how to do #1. David, explain why the group chose this answer.
Reluctant students involved	I'm glad to see everyone participating.	I'm going to ask Helen to explain #4. Help her get ready and I'll be back.
Members explaining to each other what they are learning and their reasoning processes	Great explanations! Keep it up.	I want each of you to take a problem and explain to me step-by-step how to solve it.
Group wanting to cooperate with other groups	I'm glad you're helping the other groups. Good citizenship!	Each of you go to another group and share your answer to #6.
Equal participation	Everyone is participating equally. Great group!	Rodney, you are the first to answer every time. Could you be the accuracy coach?
Groups that have finished	Your work looks good. Now do the activity written on the board.	You are being very thorough. But time is almost up. Let's speed up.
Groups working effectively	Your group is working so well. What behaviors are helping you?	Tell me what is wrong with the way this group is working. Let's make three plans to solve the problem.

Encouraging Student Self-Assessment

You can encourage self-monitoring by having each student assess how often and well she (and other group members) performed the targeted skills and actions. One way to do this is to give each group member an assessment checklist or questionnaire. These forms should ask each student for self-assessments ("I" statements) about how often and well a student performed the targeted social skills and other expected behaviors; "you" statements about how well other group members' actions were perceived as helpful or unhelpful; and "we" statements that allow group members to reach a consensus about which actions helped or hurt the group's work. Group members can then share the forms as they analyze how well they worked together.

11

Closing the Lesson

Periodically, students need to bring closure to what they are learning. We know several things about lesson closure:

1. Only students can provide closure. It happens internally, not externally.

2. Closure is an active process.

3. Closure is most effective when students can directly explain what they have learned to someone else. This requires students to formulate, conceptually organize, and summarize learning by explaining it out loud to a groupmate.

Teachers can only structure and facilitate closure; they cannot personally provide it for students. The most effective ways to facilitate closure are through focused discussion groups, writing pairs, and note-taking pairs.

At the end of a lesson, students should work in small groups (pairs or triads) to reconstruct conceptually what they were responsible for learning. Students should recall and summarize the major points in the lesson, organize the material into a conceptual framework, integrate the new information into existing conceptual frameworks, understand where they will use it in future lessons and outside the classroom, and identify final questions for the teacher. Participating in these activities immediately after a lesson increases students' retention and aids in transfer.

Focused Discussion Groups

Small, focused discussion groups are ideal for providing closure because they allow students to formulate what they know and explain it to others. Structure such focused group discussions by:

1. Having students meet in their cooperative groups (or assigning them to new groups of two or three members).

2. Giving students the task of summarizing what was covered in the lesson and what they learned. The cooperative goal is to create one paper describing what the lesson covered, the five most important things learned, and two questions about the lesson that group members wish to ask. All members must agree and be able to explain the group's work.

3. Collecting the groups' papers and recording them to support the importance of the procedure and see what students have learned. Handing the papers back periodically with brief comments helps reinforce this procedure for students.

Cooperative Writing Pairs

Organize students into pairs and ask them to work cooperatively to write a "one-minute paper" at the end of a lesson describing the major points learned and the main unanswered questions they still have. Both pair members have to agree on what is written, and both must be able to explain it. The joint writing task helps students focus on the central themes of the course and improve their writing abilities. Tell students that their papers should include:

1. An introductory paragraph outlining the content of the lesson.

2. Clear conceptual definitions of the concepts and terms presented.

3. A summary of and judgment about the material covered.

4. A description of and judgment about the practical significance of the material covered.

5. Anything the students know beyond what was covered in the lesson.

Closure Cooperative Note-Taking Pairs

Closure note-taking pairs are similar to the cooperative note-taking pairs used intermittently during the lesson (see Chapter 9). Ask the note-taking pairs to review and complete their notes, reflecting on the lesson and writing the major concepts and pertinent information presented. The cooperative goal is for students to ensure that they have a complete, comprehensive, and accurate set of notes summarizing what was covered in the lesson. Students begin by telling their partners:

1. Here is what I have in my notes.
2. Here are the key points covered in the lesson.
3. This is the most surprising idea presented by the teacher or in the material.

After each student has done this, the pairs modify their individual notes by adding anything one student had that the other did not and any new insights gained during the discussion. Students then sign each other's notes to indicate that they believe their partner's notes are complete and accurate.

Post-Lesson
Activities

12

Evaluating the Quality and Quantity of Learning

Assessing Student Learning

Assessment and evaluation are so intertwined that it's hard to separate them. But, generally, assessment involves collecting data to make a judgment, and evaluation involves judging value based on available data. Assessment does not involve assigning grades. You can have assessment without evaluation, but you cannot have evaluation without assessment.

Prior to each lesson, you must decide on the criteria you will use to evaluate student performance and plan how you will collect the information you need to make judgments. You must also define the process of learning through which students are to reach the criteria.

During the lesson, you assess student learning by observing and interviewing students (see Chapter 10 for information about observing students). You cannot measure all learning outcomes (such as level of reasoning, mastery of problem-solving procedures, metacognitive thinking) by pencil-and-paper homework assignments and tests. You can only assess these important outcomes by observing students "thinking out loud." As we discuss in Chapter 10, cooperative learning groups are "windows into students' minds," and observing these groups in action allows you to effectively assess students' work and understanding. Cooperative learning groups offer a unique opportunity for immediate diagnosis of student learning, immediate feedback from peers, and immediate remediation to correct misunderstandings and fill in gaps in students' understanding. On the basis of the information gathered during assessments, students set improvement goals and celebrate their hard work and success while you give grades.

Assessment Plans

You must make an assessment plan for each of your classes. This plan might focus on:

1. The Processes of Learning: If you are to improve continuously the quality of students' efforts to learn, you must engineer a system that assesses the processes students use to learn. According to W. Edwards Deming and other advocates of total quality management, it's important to focus on assessing and improving the processes of learning rather than to focus on outcomes. The assumption is that if you continuously improve the processes of learning, the quality and quantity of student learning will also continuously improve. This is known as total quality learning.

To implement total quality, assign students to teams, which are responsible for the quality of members' work. Team members can (a) learn how to define and organize work processes, (b) assess the quality of the processes by recording indicators of progress, and (c) place the measures on a quality chart for evaluating effectiveness.

2. The Outcomes of Learning: You must directly measure the quality and quantity of student achievement to assess how much students have actually learned in a class. Achievement has been traditionally assessed with paper-and-pencil tests. The new emphasis, however, is on assessing learning outcomes through performance measures. Performance-based assessment requires students to demonstrate what they can do with what they know by performing a procedure or skill. In a performance assessment, students complete or demonstrate the same behavior that the assessor wants to measure. Students may submit for assessment compositions, exhibitions, demonstrations, video projects, science projects, surveys, and actual job performances. When assessing student performances, you need an appropriate method of sampling the desired performances and a clearly articulated set of criteria to serve as the basis for evaluative judgments.

3. The Setting in Which Assessment Takes Place: Authentic assessment requires students to demonstrate desired skills or procedures in "real-life" contexts. Because it's impossible to place students in many real-life situations, you might want to have students complete simulated

real-life tasks or solve simulated real-life problems. To conduct an authentic assessment in science, for example, you might assign students to research teams working on a cure for cancer. They must conduct an experiment, write a lab report summarizing results, write a journal article, and make an oral presentation at a simulated convention. When conducting an authentic assessment, as well as a performance-based assessment, you need procedures for sampling performances and developing criteria for evaluation. You also need a good imagination to find real-life situations or create simulations of them.

FIGURE 12.1
Making an Assessment Plan

Performance	Process	Outcomes	Setting
Reading			
Writing			
Math Reasoning			
Presenting			
Problem Solving			
Scientific Reasoning			
Shared Leadership			
Trust Building			

Assessment Rules

There are five rules about assessment and evaluation.

Rule One: Conduct all assessment and evaluation in the context of learning teams. You must assess and evaluate each student's achievement, but the assessment is far more effective when it takes place in a team context.

Rule Two: Assess, assess, assess, and assess! Learning groups and their members need continual feedback on each member's level of learning. You should give frequent tests and quizzes and require lots of written papers and oral presentations.

Rule Three: Directly involve students in assessing each other's levels of learning. After assessments, group members should provide immediate remediation to maximize all group members' learning.

Rule Four: Use a criterion-referenced system for all assessment and evaluation. Avoid all comparisons among students' levels of achievement. Such comparison is a "force for destruction," which decreases student motivation and learning.

Rule Five: Use a wide variety of assessment formats. Cooperative learning provides an arena in which total quality learning, performance-based assessment, and authentic assessment can take place.

Following these five rules means changing current assessment and evaluation practices. The changes in assessment practices that are in schools are due to:

1. Increasing pressure to prove that schools are doing a good job (employers are unhappy with the quality of high school graduates).

2. The reexamination of education goals based on changing definitions of achievement and excellence (parents, for example, are demanding that their children receive just as good an education as students get in other countries).

3. More effective assessment options (to assess students' writing ability, we now know teachers should have students write, not answer, multiple-choice questions about sentence structure and grammar).

4. Giving teachers the responsibility for developing an assessment plan (tests provided as part of the curriculum are no longer the whole assessment package).

5. The labor-intensive nature of assessment (self-assessment and assessment by peers are needed to assess the whole range of educational outcomes).

Checking Homework

Whenever you require homework, you can use cooperative learning groups to assess the quality of each member's work and provide immediate remediation and clarification of anything the students don't understand. The task for students is to bring their completed homework to class and understand how to do it correctly. The cooperative goal is to ensure that all group members have completed their homework and understand how to do it correctly. Homework checking groups should be heterogeneous in achievement level. If you use folders for students' work, assign one member (the runner) to pick up the folders before each class and record how much of the assignment each member completed.

During each day's homework checking time, assign two students in each group to serve as Explainer and Accuracy Coach. Group members should discuss the assignment as they go through the homework answers one-by-one to ensure that they all agree on the answer and understand the information or procedures required to complete the assignment. If there is disagreement, group members should work to reach consensus. The groups should concentrate on any parts of the assignment members don't understand.

During homework checking time, as during all cooperative group activities, your role is to move from group to group listening to the explanations and answering students' questions. Also randomly ask individual students to explain how to complete their homework to ensure that there is a high degree of individual accountability.

At the end of the review time, have group members place their homework in the group's folder, which the runner returns to its proper place. Allow group members to assign each other additional homework to ensure that all group members understand the material and procedures being studied.

Giving Tests

You should frequently give tests and quizzes to assess how much each student is learning. Cooperative learning groups can be used to help prepare students for tests. Two of the purposes of testing are to evaluate how much each student knows and assess what students still need to learn. Using the following procedure achieves both purposes, provides students with immediate clarification of what they did not understand and remediation of what they did not learn, and prevents arguments between you and your students over which answers are correct and why:

1. Have students prepare for a test in cooperative learning groups. Give each cooperative group study questions and class time to prepare for the examination. The tasks are for students to discuss each study question and come to a consensus about its answer. The cooperative goal is to ensure that all group members understand how to answer the questions correctly. When the time is up, the students give each other encouragement to do well on the upcoming test.

2. Each student takes the test individually, making two copies of the answers. Students submit one set of answers to you to grade and keep

one set for the group discussion. The task (and individual goal) is to answer each test question correctly.

3. Students retake the test in their cooperative learning groups. The task again is to answer each question correctly. The cooperative goal is to ensure that all group members understand the material and procedures covered by the test. Members do so by comparing their answers on each question.

One member explains the rationale or procedure underlying each question for which there is agreement. If there is disagreement, members find the page number and paragraph explaining the relevant information or procedures and ensure that all members understand the material they missed on the test before receiving their corrected tests from the teacher. If necessary, group members assign review homework to each other. Group members should remember to celebrate how hard members have worked in learning the material and how successful they were on the test.

Assessing Oral Presentations

When you require students to give oral presentations, cooperative learning groups can serve as bookends by preparing members to give the presentation and providing a setting in which students review the effectiveness of each member's presentation. The procedure follows:

1. Assign students to cooperative learning groups.

2. Assign students (or groups) a topic or let them choose one about which they are to make a class presentation.

3. Explain to students that they are to give the presentation in a certain time frame and include visuals and active participation by the audience if you choose to require these. Also tell them that the cooperative goal is to ensure that all group members learn the material they study and develop and deliver a high-quality presentation.

4. Give students the time and resources (such as access to the library or reference materials) to prepare and rehearse their presentations. Students should make their presentation to their cooperative group and receive critical feedback at least once before they make the presentation to other members of the class.

5. Divide the class into four groups and place them in separate corners of the classroom. Have four students simultaneously make their presentations to one-fourth of the class.

6. While students listen to classmates' presentations, they should critically assess whether the individual presentations are scholarly and informative; interesting, concise, and easy to follow; engaging; and intriguing. After the presentations, students give their assessment sheets to the presenters, who take them back to their cooperative groups.

7. Sample each presentation, make your evaluation of its quality, and ask the students listening to the presentations to make a second copy of their assessments for you.

8. Have students meet in their cooperative learning groups and share their assessment sheets. The group can then make a set of recommendations on how each member can improve, which might include assigning homework and further practice presenting.

9. Be sure to have the cooperative learning groups celebrate the hard work and success of their members.

FIGURE 12.2
Quality of Oral Presentation

Criterion	Rating	Comments
Scholarly, Informative		
Interesting, Concise, Easy to Follow		
Engaging		
Intriguing		
Other:		
Other:		

For each criterion, rate the presentation from 1 (very poor) to 10 (very good).

Cooperative note-taking pairs, read and explain pairs, and math problem-solving pairs (covered in Chapter 9) can also be used for assessment.

Myths About Team-Based Assessment and Evaluation

Myth One: When You Assess Student Learning, You Have to Give Students Grades. Assessment is collecting data; giving grades is placing judgment on the students' performances. Although you can use assessment data to determine grades, improvement, not grading, is the purpose of assessment. Assessment should occur continuously with data made understandable to students so they can make judgments about how to improve.

Myth Two: You Must Read Every Student Paper and Provide Feedback. This is a destructive myth. Teachers must require more work than they can possibly judge because students need ongoing feedback for continuous improvement of learning. You alone cannot provide enough feedback on a daily basis. But with guidance and practice, students can develop the capacity to provide one another with feedback useful for improvement. This means that students must learn how to observe and collect assessment data. It does not mean that your involvement decreases. You are still responsible for carefully monitoring teamwork and intervening when appropriate to provide immediate feedback as well as providing feedback by sampling student products.

Myth Three: Students Cannot Be Meaningfully Involved in Assessment. Students are capable of assessing their own learning and the learning of their groupmates once they are taught how. Assessment skills are learned like any other skill. Students must understand why they are being asked to participate in assessment and the procedures for doing so. They must gain considerable experience in assessing learning and process how well they did. With repeated practice, students will become quite skillful in assessing their own and their groupmates' learning.

Myth Four: Involving Students in Assessment Takes Valuable Time Away from Learning and Lowers Achievement. Involving students in assessment has a number of important effects on learning that cannot be achieved any other way. Assessing the quality of groupmates' work enhances the formation of conceptual frameworks, helps students build a frame of reference for assessing the quality of their own work, promotes higher-level reasoning, and increases commitment to groupmates' learning. Far from wasting students' time, involving students in assessment is a necessary and important part of teaching.

Myth Five: Assessment is Solely a Teacher's Responsibility. You are the instructional leader in the classroom and are responsible for creating conditions that make optimal learning possible. Involving students in assessment maximizes their learning and increases their commitment to implementing improvements in learning processes.

Myth Six: Individual Assessment Suffers in Team-Based Approaches to Assessment. Team-based approaches to assessment do not eliminate the need for individual assessment. Successful teamwork comes from integrating the proficiencies of every group member to accomplish tasks that no member can accomplish alone. Assessing individual efforts enables teammates to help, assist, and support one another in the process of improvement.

13

Processing Group Effectiveness

Take care of each other. Share your energies with the group. No one must feel alone, cut off, for that is when you do not make it.
—Willi Unsoeld, Renowned Mountain Climber

Processing Starters

1. Name three things your group did well when working together. Name one thing your group could do even better.

2. Think of something each of your group members did that helped the group be effective. Tell them what it is.

3. Tell your group members how much you appreciated their help today.

4. Rate yourself from 1 (low) to 10 (high) on _____
(name a cooperative skill such as encouraging participation or checking for understanding). Share your rating with your group and explain why you rated yourself the way you did. Plan how to increase the frequency with which group members use this skill in the future.

Analyzing Group Effectiveness

Providing little or no time for students to process the quality of their cooperation is a common teaching error. Students don't learn from experiences that they don't reflect on. If learning groups are to function better tomorrow than today, students must process their work by receiving feedback, reflecting on how their actions may be more effective, and planning how to be even more skillful during future group sessions.

Group processing involves reflecting on a group session to describe which member actions were helpful in contributing to the joint efforts to achieve the group's goals and make decisions about what actions to continue or change. The purpose of group processing is to continuously improve taskwork and teamwork.

Group processing occurs at two levels—in each learning group and in the class as a whole. In small-group processing, members discuss how effectively they worked together and what could be improved. Whole-class processing involves a teacher-led discussion in which students report to the whole class what took place in their small groups.

Your role in group processing is to:

1. Ensure that each student and each group receives (and gives) feedback on the effectiveness of taskwork and teamwork.

2. Ensure that students and groups analyze and reflect on the feedback they receive.

3. Help individuals and groups set goals for improving their work.

4. Encourage the celebration of members' hard work and the group's success.

Giving and Receiving Feedback

It's important that each learning group and individual student receive feedback on the quality of their taskwork and teamwork. Feedback is information on actual performance that can be compared with criteria for ideal performance. When feedback is given skillfully, it generates energy directed toward constructive action to improve performance of skills. Feedback increases self-efficacy by helping students feel empowered to be even more effective during future tasks.

To give personal feedback in a helpful, non-threatening way (Johnson 1993):

1. Focus feedback on behaviors (not on personality traits).

2. Be descriptive (not judgmental).

3. Be specific and concrete (not general or abstract).

4. Make feedback immediate (not delayed).

5. Focus on positive actions.

6. Present feedback visually (on a graph or chart) and orally.

FIGURE 13.1
Feedback Checklist

Feedback	Yes	No, Start Over
Is feedback given?		Was not given or received. Start over.
Is feedback generating energy in students?		Students are indifferent. Start over.
Is energy directed toward identifying and solving problems so performance is improved?		Energy used to resist, deny, avoid feedback. Start over.
Do students have opportunities to take action to improve performance?		No, students are frustrated and feel like failures. Start over.

Analyzing and Reflecting on Data About Group Effectiveness

One way to help groups reflect upon and analyze their work is by plotting the observational and self-assessment data about members' interaction on a chart. The Bar Chart and the Run Chart are two of the most helpful. The following are examples of each.

FIGURE 13.2
Long-Term Group Progress: Weekly Bar Chart

Group Members: _____

_____

Class: _____ Subject Area: _____

Date: _____

On-Task Work	Contributes Ideas	Integrates/ Summarizes	Helps Groupmates	Completes Assignments

FIGURE 13.3
Long-Term Group Progress: Run Chart

Group Members: _____

_____

Class: _____ Subject Area: _____ Skill: _____

Measurement Data — Average

Time/Sequence

FIGURE 13.4
Long-Term Group Progress: Weekly Report Form

Group Members: _____

_____

Class: _____ Subject Area: _____

Date	On-Task Work	Contributes Ideas	Integrates/ Summarizes	Helps Groupmates	Completes Assignments
Totals					
Comments:					

Small-Group Processing Without Observation Data

When there are no observational data for a group to analyze or time is very short, group members can be given:

1. Thirty seconds to identify three things other members did to facilitate the group's learning.

2. A series of questions to discuss concerning their effective use of skills ("How did other group members encourage participation?" "How did other group members check for understanding?"). After each group member responds, a consensus is achieved through discussion.

3. A group-processing question as the last question on an assignment sheet. This reinforces that group processing is an integral part of learning.

Varying the procedures for processing keeps group processing vital and interesting. Other ways to structure group processing to encourage students' use of social skills include:

1. Having each group focus on one member at a time. Members tell the target person one thing he did that helped them learn or work together effectively. The focus is rotated until all members receive feedback.

2. Having members write on an index card a positive comment about each other's participation. The students can then give their written comments to each other so that every member will have written positive feedback from all other group members.

3. Having members respond to one of the following questions related to social skills for each group member:

> I appreciated it when you . . .
> I liked it when you . . .
> I admire you for your ability to . . .
> I enjoy it when you . . .
> You really helped out the group when you . . .

Students can give written responses to each other, or the procedure can be done orally. When students answer the questions face-to-face, they should be reminded to use the target person's name and make eye contact. The person receiving the positive feedback should make eye contact and say nothing or "thank you." Positive feedback should be directly and clearly expressed and should not be brushed off or denied.

4. Having each group summarize its processing and place its summary in a folder with completed academic work. This helps you stay in touch with the functioning of each learning group.

5. Having each group do a mind-map representing the elements of the group's success.

6. Having each group rate its performance on a series of dimensions on a bar chart.

Keys to successful small-group processing include allowing sufficient time for it to take place, providing a structure for processing (such as "List three things your group is doing well today and one thing you could improve"), emphasizing positive feedback, making the processing specific rather than general, maintaining student involvement in processing, reminding students to use their cooperative skills during processing, communicating clear expectations about the purpose of processing, and having group members set goals for improvement at the end of processing sessions.

Whole-Class Processing

In addition to conducting small-group processing, be sure to periodically conduct whole-class processing sessions. These sessions can be structured several ways.

1. You can share with the class the results of your observations. Charting the data to get a continuous record of class improvement is always a good idea. This lets students see how much they improved at using a particular skill over a period of time. You may wish to give a reward to the class when the total exceeds preset criteria of excellence. Not only does such a chart serve as a visual reminder of the skills students should practice while working in their groups, but it makes continuous improvement a goal that promotes class cooperation.

2. You can add together the observation results of the student observers for an overall class total. These data can also be charted.

3. You can ask students to discuss in their groups for a minute or two things they did to help each other learn and come to a consensus that they then share with the class as a whole.

Setting Improvement Goals

Goal setting is the link between how students did today and how well they will do tomorrow. After analyzing observation and self-assessment data, reflecting on their meaning, and giving each other feedback, group members must set improvement goals specifying how they will act more skillfully in the future. Students should publicly announce the behavior they plan to improve, and the goal should be written down and reviewed at the beginning of the next group session.

Goal setting has a powerful effect on students' behavior by providing a sense of ownership of and commitment to actions students have decided to engage in (as opposed to assigned behaviors). The following are a few ways you can structure goal setting:

1. Have students set specific behavioral goals for the next group session. Have each student pick a specific social skill to use more effectively (an "I" focus), or have the group reach a consensus about which collaborative skill all group members will work on in the next session (a "we" focus). Consider requiring groups to hand in a written statement specifying which social skill each member is going to emphasize during the next work session. This helps keep you informed about group functioning.

2. In a whole-class processing session, ask each group to agree on one conclusion to the statement, "Our group could do better on social skills by . . . ," and tell their answer to the entire class. Write the answers on the board under the title "Goals." At the beginning of the next cooperative learning lesson, read over the goal statements and remind students what they agreed to work on during the session.

3. Have each student write an answer to one of the following questions after a cooperative learning session:

   a. "Something I plan to do differently next time to help my group is . . ."
   b. "The social skill I want to use next time is . . ."
   c. "I can help my group next time by . . ."
   d. "The things I will do to help my group next time are . . ."
   e. "One social skill I will practice more consistently next time is . . ."

4. Have students plan where, outside of class, they can apply the social skills they are learning in class. This is an optional activity and helps them make connections between cooperative learning and other areas of their lives. "I" and "we" focuses are useful in this assignment.

Celebrating

Group processing ends with students celebrating their hard work and the success of their cooperative learning groups. Small-group and whole-class celebrations are key to encouraging students to persist in their efforts to learn (Johnson and Johnson 1993). Feeling successful, appreciated, and respected builds commitment to learning, enthusiasm about working in cooperative groups, and a sense of self-efficacy about subject matter mastery and working cooperatively with classmates. Being recognized for efforts to learn and to contribute to groupmates' learning reaches the heart far more effectively than grades or tangible rewards; long-term, hard, persistent efforts to learn come more from the heart than from the head.

Obstacles to Group Processing

The following are some common obstacles to group processing (Dishon and O'Leary 1984). For each obstacle, a number of solutions are suggested.

1. Too little time for group processing. For many reasons (fire drills, announcements, assemblies, discipline problems), teachers often believe they cannot make time for group processing. If you feel this way, think about:

a. Doing quick processing by rapidly asking the class to tell how well their groups are functioning. You can do this by making a statement and then having students indicate agreement or disagreement: agree (hand in air), don't know (arms folded), disagree (hands down). Two or three statements can be made and responded to in a minute or so.

b. Doing processing and having students finish the work at home or the next day in class.

2. Processing stays vague. When students conclude, "We did okay," "We did a good job," or "Everyone was involved," you know that the processing is not specific enough. Some suggested remedies are:

a. Use specific statements to which students must give detailed responses.

b. Use student observers to record the appearance of specific behaviors.

3. Students stay uninvolved in processing. Occasionally there will be groups whose members consistently stay uninvolved in analyzing the group's functioning. In such a case, try:

a. Asking for a written report from the group about the strengths and weaknesses of their functioning.

b. Using processing sheets that require participation from everyone.

c. Assigning the student least involved in the processing the job of recorder or spokesperson for the group.

d. Having all members sign the processing statement to indicate they participated in the group processing and agree with the group's conclusions.

e. Giving bonus points for group processing reports.

4. Incomplete or messy written process reports. Some groups might hand in incomplete or messy reports of their group processing. If so, you might try:

a. Having group members sign each other's processing sheets to show that each has been checked for completeness and neatness.

b. Giving bonus points for neatness and completeness.

5. Poor cooperative skills used during processing. When group members don't listen carefully to each other, are afraid to contribute to the processing, or angrily disagree, you might intervene by:

a. Assigning specific roles during processing.

b. Having one group member observe the processing and asking the group to discuss the results.

14

Final Words

Cooperative learning is the instructional use of small groups so that students work together to maximize their own and each other's learning. The essence of cooperative learning involves using formal cooperative learning groups, informal cooperative learning groups, and cooperative base groups to make students positively interdependent so they recognize that they "sink or swim" together. Other basic elements of cooperation include individual accountability (every student is accountable for both learning the assigned material and helping other group members learn), face-to-face promotive interaction among students (students promote each other's success), interpersonal and small-group skills, and student processing of how effectively their learning groups function.

Research provides exceptionally strong evidence that cooperation results in greater effort to achieve, more positive interpersonal relationships, and greater psychological health than competitive or individualistic learning efforts. As a teacher using cooperative learning, you will have to carefully plan and perform four specific actions. First, you must make a number of pre-instructional decisions. You must decide on your academic and social skills objectives; what size groups to use, how to assign students to groups, and how long the groups will work together; how best to arrange your classroom; how you will use instructional materials; and which roles to assign the group members.

Second, you must explain to students what they are to do during the cooperative lesson. You must give a clear academic assignment and explain the positive interdependence in and between groups, the individual accountability, and what teamwork skills are to be emphasized during each lesson so they can continuously improve.

Third, you must conduct the lesson. While students work together cooperatively, you must monitor the learning groups and intervene (when needed) to improve their taskwork and teamwork. And you must be sure to help students provide closure to the lesson.

Finally, you must structure post-lesson activities. Academic learning must be assessed and evaluated. Students must process how effectively they and their learning groups functioned during each lesson so they can continuously improve.

One of the things we've been told many times by teachers who have mastered the use of cooperative learning is, "Don't say it's easy!" We know it's not. It can take years to become an expert. And there's a lot of pressure to teach like everyone else, to have students learn alone, and not to let students look at each other's papers. Students themselves will not be accustomed to working together and are likely to have a competitive orientation. Our advice is to start small by using cooperative learning for one topic or in one class until you feel comfortable, and then expand its use into other topics or classes. Implementing cooperative learning in your classroom takes disciplined effort. It's not easy. But it's worth the effort.

References

Aronson, E. (1978). *The Jigsaw Classroom.* Beverly Hills, Calif.: Sage Publications.

Deutsch, M. (1949). "A Theory of Cooperation and Competition." *Human Relations* 2: 129–152.

DeVries, D., and K. Edwards. (1974). "Student Teams and Learning Games: Their Effects on Cross-Race and Cross-Sex Interaction." *Journal of Educational Psychology* 66: 741–749.

Dishon, D., and P. O'Leary. (1984). *A Guidebook for Cooperative Learning.* Holmes Beach, Fla.: Learning Publications.

Johnson, D.W. (1979). *Educational Psychology.* Englewood Cliffs, N.J.: Prentice-Hall.

Johnson, D.W. (1991). *Human Relations and Your Career* (3rd ed.). Englewood Cliffs, N.J.: Prentice-Hall.

Johnson, D.W. (1993). *Reaching Out: Interpersonal Effectiveness and Self-Actualization* (6th ed.). Needham Heights, Mass.: Allyn & Bacon.

Johnson, D.W., and F. Johnson. (1994). *Joining Together: Group Theory and Group Skills* (5th ed.). Needham Heights, Mass.: Allyn & Bacon.

Johnson, D.W., and R. Johnson. (1989). *Cooperation and Competition: Theory and Research.* Edina, Minn.: Interaction Book Company.

Johnson, D.W., and R. Johnson. (1991). *Teaching Students To Be Peacemakers.* Edina, Minn.: Interaction Book Company.

Johnson, D.W., and R. Johnson. (1992). *Creative Controversy: Intellectual Challenge in the Classroom.* Edina, Minn.: Interaction Book Company.

Johnson, D.W., and R. Johnson. (1993). *Leading the Cooperative School* (2nd ed.). Edina, Minn.: Interaction Book Company.

Johnson, D.W., and R. Johnson. (1975/1994). *Learning Together and Alone: Cooperative, Competitive, and Individualistic Learning.* Englewood Cliffs, N.J.: Prentice-Hall.

Johnson, D.W., R. Johnson, and E. Holubec. (1983). *Circles of Learning* (videotape). Edina, Minn.: Interaction Book Company.

Johnson, D.W., R. Johnson, and E. Holubec. (1992). *Advanced Cooperative Learning.* Edina, Minn.: Interaction Book Company.

Johnson, D.W., R. Johnson, and E. Holubec. (1993). *Cooperation in the Classroom* (6th ed.). Edina, Minn.: Interaction Book Company.

Johnson, D.W., R. Johnson, and K. Smith. (1991). *Active Learning: Cooperation in the College Classroom*. Edina, Minn.: Interaction Book Company.

Johnson, R., and D.W. Johnson. (1985). *Warm-ups, Grouping Strategies, and Group Activities*. Edina, Minn.: Interaction Book Company.

Kagan, S. (1988). *Cooperative Learning*. San Juan Capistrano, Calif.: Resources for Teachers.

Katzenbach, J., and D. Smith. (1993). *The Wisdom of Teams*. Cambridge, Mass.: Harvard Business School Press.

Kouzes, J., and B. Posner. (1987). *The Leadership Challenge*. San Francisco: Jossey-Bass.

Sharan, S., and Y. Sharan. (1976). *Small-group Teaching*. Englewood Cliffs, N.J.: Educational Technology Publications.

Stevenson, H., and J. Stigler. (1992). *The Learning Gap*. New York: Summit.